The New Job Success Guide and Journal Copy

The Proven One-Year Model to Accelerate Your Career

Mike Manoske

Crystal Cove Media

Crystal Cove Media

© Copyright 2024 All rights reserved.

Legal Notice:

The content contained within this book may not be reproduced, duplicated or transmitted without direct written permission from the author or the publisher.

Under no circumstances will any blame or legal responsibility be held against the publisher, or author, for any damages, reparation, or monetary loss due to the information contained within this book, either directly or indirectly.

This book is copyright protected. It is only for personal use. You cannot amend, distribute, sell, use, quote or paraphrase any part, or the content within this book, without the consent of the author or publisher.

ISBN Ebook 978-1-7370180-4-9

ISBN Paperback 978-1-7370180-5-6

ISBN Hardback 978-1-7370180-6-3

Cover design by Yayun Chang-Cahill

Free Journal and Staying Connected

Click here to sign up for my newsletter on Job, Career and Leadership. As a thank you, I'll send you a free spreadsheet of New Job Success Journal built for an entire year. Click here sign up: mikecoach.com/newjobjournal

Book Reviews are the core of a author's success. Take a moment to do this. I am grateful for all the feedback. It boosts the popularity of the book by helping other readers with their careers. Here are the links:

Amazon US| Amazon Canada | Amazon UK | Amazon Germany | Amazon France | Amazon Spain | Amazon Netherlands

Contents

1. Introduction — 3
2. Demonstrate and Deliver Value — 8
3. Fast Learning — 23
4. Building Relationships — 37
5. The 5 Challenges Overview — 53
6. Success — 58
7. Failure — 66
8. Dealing with Conflict — 72
9. Ambiguity — 79
10. Prioritization and Negotiation — 88
11. Presence and Brand — 97
12. The Balancing Act — 103
13. Journaling — 114
14. Conclusion — 142
15. Acknowledgements — 145
16. References — 146
17. About the Author — 149
18. A Final Word on Reviews — 150

NEW JOB SUCCESS MODEL

 THE GAME PLAN

 THE 5 CHALLENGES

 DEVELOPING EXPERTISE

Introduction

Even though I'm a long time career and executive coach, I've shared a common challenge with my clients: the excitement and anxiety of starting a new job. These feelings, which I've seen in the thousands of people I've hired during my two decades as a Recruiting Leader and in the classroom as a co-leader of the Job Search Action Group program at the Wharton Business School, are universal. It's this shared experience that has driven me to write this book, to offer guidance and support during this critical transition.

While there are a few books that address the challenges of starting a new role for non-C-level executives, they often focus on the short-term, the first few months. This book takes a different approach. It's designed to provide models and strategies that can help a wider audience, covering the critical first year and beyond, offering a comprehensive guide to long-term success in a new role.

In the early days of my coaching practice, I helped people land new roles, and I still do to this day. I blend coaching, recruiting, and hiring manager experience to assist with job search logistics and the emotional rollercoaster it can trigger. I co-wrote my first book, The Job Search Manifesto, with Steve Hernandez based on the program we developed at Wharton. It fills an important need in the marketplace and ends with signing the offer letter. I quickly found out that my clients wanted more.

More and more clients kept me on to help them navigate the new job. Much of my practice now focuses on succeeding in a new role and career success. Seeing the many methods, tools, and ideas my clients and I used in their new job success was the catalyst for this book.

New Job success is a unique interaction that aligns your work and focus with the organization's needs. I have witnessed transformational impact when a client successfully met that alignment and delivered solid, consistent results. But it doesn't typically happen in three months; it takes time to gain the skills, knowledge, and mastery to provide value. In fact, there is a common four-stage learning process we follow: Conscious Competence.

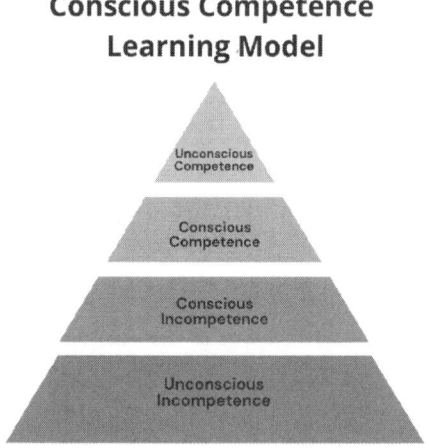

1. **Unconscious Incompetence**

2. is the starting point. We are unaware we do something poorly.

3. **Conscious Incompetence** happens when we know we don't do a task well. This stage often triggers improvement.

4. **Conscious Competence** is a critical stage that results from an effort to improve. The task or work gets done, though it's not automatic.

5. **Unconscious Competence** is when the work can be done effortlessly or in a flow state.

This book aims to give you the tools to move your job into a state of Competence, with some work done at a level of unconscious Competence. This takes time, effort, and, most importantly, a plan. The New Job Success Guide and Journal offers that plan.

The book is laid out in three parts to help you build your confidence and Competence along with early wins. Here are the three parts:

The Game Plan

This is an essential part of your new job success. You focus on three tracks of action: **demonstrating and delivering value**, **fast learning**, and **building relationships**. These are the core activities that drive success in a new role. This section gives you a plan to execute on your first day and into your new job's first three to four months. The Game Plan helps you spend more time executing and less time being unsure. The Game Plan enables you to become competent.

The Five Challenges

As you move into your new job, everyday speed bumps come up. Most organizations ask about some or all of them in the interview process. We interview them because they are almost inevitable.

Understanding how you deal with them, including the frameworks and methods you use to address them, is key. The section on five challenges looks at **success, failure, conflict, ambiguity, prioritization, and negotiation**.

This book section offers best practices and tools for dealing with these challenging areas. It prepares you to be ready for each of these areas and be aware of the situation.

Developing Expertise

Managing the Game Plan activity tracks and dealing with the five challenges helps you develop more skills and experiences: you are growing and maximizing your growth, and the focus of this section keying in on: your **presence and brand** and **the balancing act**. These two areas aim to keep you balanced and authentic with a healthy foundation for your life. This is when you are unconsciously competent with some of your work.

New Job Success Journal

This is a unique and essential part of this book. I wanted to give you a way to document your experience and base it on the sections I'm presenting. Journaling is an effective way to gain insight, even more so with an easy-to-use structure. The journal in this book uses bullet journaling that takes less time and makes it easy to spot trends and patterns.

I want this book to position you for success. When you begin at your new organization, you are seen as the new person, and leaders will develop assumptions about you—that's just how humans are. However, when you go in with realistic and clear expectations and communicate them, you set yourself up for a positive experience.

The framework in this book has helped thousands of clients, and much of it came from clients themselves. Like any good coach, I captured the methods that work, and I'm sharing them here.

I don't want you to think of this book as something you read once and move on. It is also a reference book, where you can come back to it and examine the areas you want to further develop or deal with when challenges come up.

In his book Outliers, Malcolm Gladwell proposes that 10,000 hours are needed to master a skill. Much of your work will not require mastery, but excelling at something takes time and persistence. With all this said, it is time to dive into what matters- succeeding in your new role.

Demonstrate and Deliver Value

Game Plan Track 1

Scenario

The new organization you just joined was welcoming and your onboarding was well organized and thorough. In initial discussions with your boss and team members, they make multiple comments about how much you are needed and there's a lot of work coming.

Yet, when asked for specifics, you only get vague answers. Your new leader says, "Get settled in and then we'll go over your work plan." You feel excitement but also a sense of discomfort. The lack of clarity even in the first few days of starting creates some anxiety on your part. To compensate, you say Yes to multiple tasks and projects but start to lose track of those commitments. Some deadlines are missed, and you find the core part of your work is not getting done.

To meet and exceed expectations, we often overcompensate by taking on a lot right up front; that's the theme in this Chapter's scenario. I've also seen another approach: a new employee being too passive and holding back, taking an observer stance versus taking much action. I see clients make these common missteps, and they do so with the best of intentions: they want to be successful. Taking too much action or too little action are self-defeating approaches. This Chapter covers a better alternative, a mix of planning, delivering wins, and building on those to create more wins and value. It's a model to work smarter. Those who work smarter are the ones who are more likely to succeed. But remember that working smarter has nothing to do with being lazy; it is efficiency, getting more done in less time.

How you perform is important, but your results—how the impact of your work is perceived and measured—are far more critical. In this Chapter, I'll discuss how to outline a system that ensures you show and deliver value every time while making your transition to a new environment more accessible.

Shiny Objects and KPI's

There are lots of approaches to measuring the value that you deliver. Still, **key performance indicators (KPIs)** are a great way to track your progress and performance. I'll cover a few ways, but before we get that, there's a common trait to stay aware of: **"shiny object syndrome"** or SOS. This is a challenge where individuals become easily distracted about something exciting or new, or, to refer to the name of the syndrome, shiny. These can be projects, ideas, or opportunities, often leading to a need for more commitment or focus on current goals. Understanding how shiny objects affect you will help you set successful KPIs.

Shiny object syndrome commonly triggers distraction. People with SOS shift their focus or attention from one project or idea to another without finishing the first one. There's also a need for follow-through where the individual might start multiple projects but never reach completion, leaving a trail of unfinished endeavors. SOS is also associated with impulsive decision-making. SOS sufferers often decide without proper research or evaluation of their feasibility or risks. This usually leads to an overcommitment, taking on too many projects, which frequently makes them feel overwhelmed and decreases their effectiveness.

There's usually a short-lived enthusiasm in people who suffer from SOS, where they get incredibly excited about something new, but it wanes quickly. These "symptoms" often lead to inconsistent results on the individual's behalf, not only in one area but in many. Why am I telling you about this? SOS can hinder your professional growth, preventing you from dedicating the time and effort you need to excel at the goals you have set for yourself first. You must have well-defined roadmaps that keep temptation at bay and ensure you stay on track. And this is where KPIs come in handy.

KPIs can help minimize SOS. KPIs act as a barometer for delivering value in your new role if set up well. Here's a great definition of KPI's:

"A Key Performance Indicator (KPI) is a measurable target that indicates how individuals or businesses meet their goals. Reviewing and evaluating KPIs helps organizations determine whether or not they are on track for hitting their desired objectives." (Hennigan, L. 2023)

Let's take the definition and start applying it to your new job.

The Demonstrating and Delivering Value Model

Throughout this book, I'll offer models that have been successful for many of my clients. They are broken down into actionable, smaller steps to improve your ability to implement them. Here are the four steps in the demonstrate and deliver value model.

DEMONSTRATE AND DELIVER VALUE

1. Develop job-specific KPIs

2. Develop career KPIs

3. Regular status reports to leaders and teams

4. Track, assess, and iterate the plan

Achieving success in your new job can be challenging when you immediately immerse yourself in tasks without first grasping the essential knowledge. Don't get me wrong, the enthusiasm for securing early victories can bring success to the new job. However, plunging into action without clearly understanding what makes up a "win" within the new organization can jeopardize your aspirations for rapid development. Therefore, when entering a new organization, success often comes from two distinct things: **achieving the right things** and **communicating those achievements** effectively.

Step 1: Develop Job-Specific KPIs

A core principle is to be data-driven and avoid subjectivity with your work output. KPIs create data-driven clarity for you, your boss, and anyone affected by your work. They take some effort to make, but will ultimately save you hours of wasted effort, concern about meeting expectations, and establish strong bonds in the organization. How can you identify which KPI you should choose within your organization? It would help if you didn't rely on intuition alone for this, as it often demands a systematic approach where you consistently apply minimal margins for errors.

I've found three questions to narrow the most crucial KPI among other KPIs. The first is, **what KPI would be most relevant to your organization's core objectives?** Identifying KPIs that align with your organization's core goals is crucial because it can significantly affect your performance and the organization's. Focusing on the proper KPI can help your progress and cloud potential opportunities.

good yeilds, Clean Space, organized lobooks

Answering that question requires four pieces of information:

Precision: where the KPI should be quantifiable, and current performances should be measured as accurately as possible. This means the more detailed the measures, the more effective they become.

Targets and timelines: set numeric targets and establish clear timelines to achieve them. Without a target or a deadline, you lack the driving force needed to continue to progress. *[handwritten: yeild %]* *[handwritten: Processing my experiments by Self by end of month]*

High-quality data: Make sure your chosen KPI relies on objective and clean data sources. Consistency in data collection is crucial for ongoing performance tracking. *[handwritten: → organized Lobnotebook / Calculation]*

Differentiate between leading and lagging KPIs: Leading KPIs focus on future outcomes or states, like aiding in shaping strategies or predicting future sales. Lagging KPIs include percentage changes in past-month sales or measuring past performances. Understanding the distinction between these two will help you adjust your strategy.

The next question: **can you vouch for the quality of the chosen KPIs?** Selecting KPIs without assessing them is a common mistake. To avoid this, make sure your KPIs meet the following criteria. They should be:

Within your control, it measures what you direct versus trying to manage external factors you have limited sway over.

Relevant and directly relate to the organizational goals. Avoid overly complicated KPIs that might hamper your team's understanding of them.

Measurable. As mentioned above, high-quality KPIs must be accurate with consistent numerical measurements.

Contribute to the organization's overall progress, not just specific areas like finance or sales.

If you manage a team, consider designating certain team members responsible for a KPI.

This leads to the next and final question: **Who will own each KPI?** Usually, you are eager to take on multiple responsibilities in your new role, but effective KPI management often requires delegation. While assigning duties to your team members is common, it might be challenging, especially as you are new and building trust. However, start with a KPI that you can fully manage and avoid the pitfall of taking on too much too soon. As a manager, you are ultimately responsible for completing each KPI, but delegating some or all of the work is an intelligent use of time and resources.

Step 2: Develop Career KPIs

Establishing KPIs within the organization is a foundational step. Still, it is only one milestone in your journey toward career success. What's intriguing is that you have the exclusive authority to shape your path. However, your power to navigate it lies in your proactive approach—career KPIs.

KPIs are more commonly associated with organizations and businesses, but you can use them personally. After all, they can be any measurable variable that you can use to channel and enhance your productivity. While job-specific KPIs are those you collaborate on with your team, career KPIs are metrics you can employ to evaluate your personal growth. Once again, it would help if you posed similar coaching questions but with a notable distinction. In an organization, the overarching goals are almost always established. With career KPIs, you have the privilege of setting goals from scratch. Here are three questions I often use in my practice to build Career KPIs

What is your vision for your career?

Finding Joy in expureinces made

Where do you envision yourself in one, two, and five years or the future?

Leading a team

What is your "why"? What makes this vision significant to you, and what does it represent?

I Like working as a team to keep the company Like a well oiled meschme

These questions take time, but like the rest of this Chapter, it's a sound investment. Once you have answered those questions, enrich them with additional criteria, such as those we discussed earlier. Are your Career KPIs controllable, measurable, understandable, and relevant to your vision? Do they encompass sufficient diversity to capture your career's overall growth trajectory?

As long as your chosen KPIs align with these criteria, you have the flexibility to either create your own or build from these suggested categories:

Financial: This category is the most tangible, encompassing metrics such as salary, benefits, variable pay, and rewards. Investments can also be a part.

Work-life balance: This encompasses hours worked, vacation days, remote work flexibility, and stress levels. We look at this further in the Chapter on the Balancing Act.

Prospect for growth: Evaluate the potential for advancement within your current role in the organization, evaluate the opportunities for learning new skills, the availability of mentorship programs, and the extent to which your current position allows you to expand your professional network.

Job satisfaction: Here, you look at the level of engagement you have with your daily tasks and responsibilities, how often you get feedback and recognition, the alignment between your values and the organization's culture, and the quality of your relationship with colleagues.

Career status: This revolves around your progress regarding job title and position, which show career advancement; tracking salary increases and bonuses; evaluating how your responsibilities have developed; and industry recognition such as awards, certifications, or any other recognitions.

Meaning, purpose, and values: Here, you would assess how closely your job aligns with your values and sense of purpose, the positive impact you feel you make in your role, and whether your current position aligns with your long-term career goals.

Learning and Development: This encompasses evaluating your access to professional development opportunities, tracking the acquisition of new knowledge and skills, assessing the quality and frequency of feedback from those above you, and measuring challenging tasks that encourage continuous learning.

Building personal KPIs is a process you don't do once but revisit frequently. Aim to keep them fresh, relevant, and motivating.

Step 3: Regular Reports to Leaders and Teams

Delivering status reports to leaders and teams should be a baseline activity. First, it is a way for you to get noticed not only by yourself but also by your work, as well as contribute visibly to leaders and team members. This visibility can help others realize what you are working on and how your efforts align with the rest of the team and the company's goals. Not only that, but all employers are accountable for something, and you can further prove that by sending regular status reports. It shows leaders and others that you take your role seriously and are committed to delivering results. It helps you improve your communication when you regularly prepare and send status reports, such as helping you articulate your progress and challenges. Communication is a core to new job success and will often come up in this book.

You can use status reports to clarify your expectations with those above you and your team. At the start, you are expected to have doubts about specific goals the organization or team wants to achieve or any other uncertainties you might have, which you documented in your report and potentially addressed. But you can also see this as a way of tracking goals, which, by definition, allows you to identify areas where you can improve and take steps to increase that particular "flaw." Again, there might be some uncertainty when you work with a new team, and your goals need to align with the team's goals. However, status reports help align those goals and show how your work contributes to the team's goals.

Finally, consistently sharing well-written and well-structured status reports shows your commitment and transparency. Colleagues and leaders understand your workload, progress, and any challenges you are facing.

These reports can be done and structured in different ways, need certain aspects to make them legit and understandable. Start with your publishing schedule. **How regular will your reports be?** You can choose from weekly, biweekly, or monthly reports, but factor in the organization's reporting schedule.

You must know **what type of information you provide in the report.** Identify essential details that comprise key achievements, milestones, progress updates, plans, and any challenges you have found. You have already specified the KPIs, so use those to measure and ensure they align with the project's goals. When creating the report, you might have to gather some data, so you must ensure the data is accurate, relevant, and up-to-date for the report.

When structuring the reports, make them **clear, concise, and consistent**. The most common sections are KPIs, risks and challenges, actions, an executive summary, or a timeline. Of course, you can work on these, and it all depends on context, which you should always provide. This is especially true when presenting information. Explain how the current status aligns with the project's goals and why some challenges and milestones matter more. Ideally, you'd use graphs, charts, and other visuals to make the report cleaner and easier to read, mainly if you use more complex data.

Please **address any challenges or risks** that might have come up and communicate what these entail and how they might have affected any methods or strategies you have put in place. In the same way, highlight **your achievements,** but always recognize any team effort and any other contributions that made those accomplishments possible. Last, you should add any recommendations or insights you see fit. You can add potential solutions to any challenges or ideas for any improvements.

In Step 4, I'll discuss a reporting approach you might use.

Step 4: Track, Assess, and Iterate the Plan

It's simple: you need to tell others what you are doing. This is especially important for a new employee; you need to show and deliver value. Here are some steps to reporting effectively.

For tracking, one of the main things to highlight is skill development and competencies. When you do this, you can quickly identify which skills are crucial for your role and how your proficiency in those skills is improving. It also allows you to track progress toward specific goals that align with the company's priorities and contribute to delivering value. In the same way, track challenges, as I have stated above, when doing regular status reports, but mainly so you can identify any obstacles that might hinder value delivery. Tracking your overall performance and contributions over time can help you see the positive results your work creates for your team and the organization.

Regular assessments of goal attainment allow you to fully understand whether you're on track to meet your goals and ensure that your efforts align with the organization's goals. Similarly, assessing challenges that come your way allows you to understand any impact these obstacles or issues might have on your delivery of value and find out if you need help or if you need to find other solutions. The other factor is noting how others respond to your reports. What are they taking away from them—and is that what you intended?

Based on the assessments, iterate your improvements through the investment in skills through training, workshops, or even mentorship. This can fast-track value to the organization and team. After assessment and tracking, if you know that you are falling short on some goals or are not contributing to what you have expected, you can adjust your methods and strategies through an iterative process that ensures you stay focused on value delivery. By optimizing value through iterations, you improve your workflow and processes and find more efficient ways to do your job.

For new employees, the track, assess, and iterate plan is a great way to align skills with goals and enhance performance. By continually doing this, you can improve and actively show that you are delivering value.

Communicating the Reports

You have done the report, but how do you communicate it? There are two methods, and you can use both written and verbal. By doing both, they must be in sync and support each other well. Many of my clients use stoplight reports because it is a quick way to summarize the status and easily highlight what's going well, potential issues, and more significant issues that might hinder progress. I used this type of report early in my career as an engineering manager. I continued using it once I transitioned into recruiting, leadership, and coaching. Many of my clients, whether they work for a Fortune 500 company or a startup, use the stoplight report. For instance, to keep stakeholders informed, one of my clients attaches a screenshot of his stoplight report in a weekly email, where he includes a status column in green, amber, or red, and he has nothing but appreciation from the stakeholders because it is easy to understand. But you might need to be fully aware of a stoplight report, so I'll break it down for you.

The stoplight or RAG (red, amber, green) report is a way to communicate effectively in writing. It is especially helpful when reporting on a project or its status, as well as KPIs. As you might have guessed, it uses color-coded indicators (green, amber, and red) to create a visual aid about the status of the different sections and elements of the report.

As I have said, a stoplight report adds visual clarity through color coding, further explaining and simplifying the complex information it might have in the report. This allows readers to see the statuses of the report's different sections without having to dive into the text. This gives immediate recognition through the colors presented, which are universal—green shows a positive status, amber shows a warning or potential problem, and red suggests an actual problem.

This type of report directs attention to critical areas that require immediate attention, prioritizing the readers' focus on what section needs more attention. It allows readers to understand the entire report at a glance, which is especially important if they have to make quick decisions based on the report. This makes these types of reports concise by providing essential information that is also detailed if the reader delves into the text.

For instance, amber indicators allow for early issue detection and risk mitigation, which might prompt addressing potential issues before they become more critical (red).

Depending on the report's context, stoplight reports can also provide an objective way to assess performance or progress against a benchmark and track trends. The change of colors provides a visual aid with performance trends, making it easier to identify improvements or other areas where improvements are needed.

When communicating verbally, remember that it has to be in sync with and support the written report. I want to discuss three methods of verbally communicating here: radical candor, crucial conversations, and nonviolent communication.

Radical Candor

You can look at this method as a framework that encourages open and honest communication while demonstrating care for the receiver. It allows you to give clear and direct feedback when presenting your report and recommendations to ensure that the person you are reporting to fully understands the message. This method also emphasizes active listening on your behalf when reporting it to understand any responses from the receiver so you can respond more empathetically to their concerns. You must engage in the conversation with care while providing the report, especially if you report it to a manager and express concerns about their goals.

Crucial Conversations

This different verbal communication approach allows you to deliver high-stakes and emotionally charged conversations more effectively. Like radical candor, it allows for open dialogue but also mutual understanding. It is vital that when reporting, you are in a safe space, but this method promotes this type of environment. Here, you can use information that leads to different perspectives or views, and this method encourages you to explore these differences constructively while seeking the receiver's point of view. When discussing the report, make sure you retain the focus of the conversation and focus on the shared goals and outcomes you want to achieve so you can reach productive solutions.

Nonviolent Communication

Also known as NVC, nonviolent communication is an approach that empowers you to communicate with empathy while expressing your needs compassionately. The goal of this method is mainly to resolve conflicts and encourage understanding without resorting to judgment. So, focus on empathic communication and empathic listening. This encompasses active listening to your manager's or your team's response and empathizing with their perspective and concerns. Here, you're using nonjudgmental observations of the facts and framing feedback and observations to reduce defensiveness. So, in sum, NVC can better apply to express your needs. Still, other aspects, such as requests for collaborations or action, can be requested through this method.

Any of these methods offers you different tools for effectively conveying a report, even if it is to support your written report. Choosing the right one depends on the context, but any of the three can lead to constructive conversations that help your written report and ensure collaboration, understanding, and more efficient decision-making. We'll also revisit these methods in the Chapter on Conflict.

Summary

So, now that you know the steps to deliver value, you need to execute a process. First, you write it down (for instance, through a stoplight report). Here, you document your goals and KPIs to achieve. Writing the objectives allows you to provide clarity and accountability, setting clear expectations for the reader.

Then, discuss it through a verbal report, where you will discuss the contents of the written report with the manager or whoever you are reporting to. While this discussion can take place in different settings, one-on-one meetings or group meetings are preferable. Verbal reporting gives a deeper understanding of the goals and progress and clarifies any relevant issues. This ensures alignment regarding objectives and can be a good way to receive or provide feedback or share insights.

The third step is to adjust for outside forces. Commonly, organizations change priorities, market conditions change, and team members and other personnel come or leave. These are all external factors that can affect goals and objectives. That is why you adjust to these outside forces and ensure the goals remain relevant and achievable. Adjustments also make it more efficient and avoid wasting resources on goals that might no longer contribute value to the organization.

The last step is taking action and continuing to deliver goals. Take action after you have set goals, discussed them, and adjusted them to any external forces. You and the team must continue working toward achieving the goals. You can see this step as execution, where you implement action plans and make progress.

In the following Chapter, I'm going to discuss an essential tool vital to your success in your new job: fast learning. We will discuss all the steps for you to learn quickly and efficiently so that you can adapt to your new job with ease.

Fast Learning

Game Plan Track 2

Scenario

You knew when you accepted the offer there were several areas that would be new to you, and you'd have to ramp up. This organization has processes that are more involved than you've had experience with. They also are using tools that are new to you. Learning the tools is important since much of the project tracking is done through them.

One reason you joined was to work with larger teams on strategy and planning. This is a step up for you; previous roles had you executing the work, but not much design. Planning and working with larger teams is a great step for you, but you need to learn more about the functions and interplay between your new team and the others.

You'll need some level of understanding of the other team's operations and how your work syncs with theirs. Becoming conversant in this is an important new area to learn.

All this learning on processes, tools, planning and functions feels challenging, and you want to be thoughtful about the best ways to learn and execute in your new role.

Fast Learning is a well-rounded and more detailed approach than just randomly "learning on the job." In that old model, you were supposed to learn through observation and repetition. That works well when the job focuses on procedural tasks that are narrow and well-defined. However, work has grown to include decision-making and multiple outcomes, requiring more profound knowledge. Fast Learning considers this, and the following approaches and models aim to help you with the everyday challenges described in this chapter's scenario.

Fast Learning aims to improve your retention of essential knowledge and then apply the information in your work. There are four steps to implement, and they are not linear. Your learning style and the content you must understand will guide your approach. Incorporating these action steps will boost your Learning:

1. **Assess and focus:** This is where you identify any knowledge gaps and find resources to gain this knowledge.

2. **Study and review:** This is where you build a plan that fits how you learn. You want to learn in chunks to create small wins to build on.

3. **Validate and repeat:** You frequently check that your Learning is on the right track and adjust your process as needed.

4. **Level of knowledge:** You determine the expertise required for specific tasks.

Assess and Focus

This initial step identifies knowledge gaps that you might have and finds the resources to fill in those gaps.

Start this step with a detailed **self-assessment of your knowledge and other related skills**. The method for doing this can vary, but you can inventory existing expertise, coursework, or prior experiences to identify what you know and don't.

Once you know what is missing from your knowledge, you must set goals. Essentially, think about what you aim to achieve by filling these gaps. **How will you apply the knowledge in your new role?** Having clear and defined goals will provide you with a sense of direction and motivate you.

Next, you must **find the best resources** with the information you need. Nowadays, we have access to many resources, but only some are useful. It is essential that you choose your resources carefully and that, while doing so, you consider their reliability, credibility, and relevance to the subject at hand. Such resources include textbooks, academic papers, online courses, or even mentors in the field. Often, the knowledge source may be a person in the organization considered the "go-to person" in a particular area.

The last step is to **allocate time to learning these knowledge gaps.** Ideally, you'll create a schedule outlining when to engage with the chosen resources. Regardless of the time spent, it would help to be consistent with your routine.

Study and Review

The primary method here is not to read lengthy papers with a lot of information to keep from them but **to learn in small chunks** to absorb the information more easily. While it might all belong to a single topic, you must break down complex information and issues into smaller, more manageable chunks.

When studying, you can focus on one chunk of information at a time. But your engagement with the material must be active while you do that. You give total attention to the information by summarizing the main points and taking notes, for example, because this will improve knowledge retention.

There's a technique that I highly recommend while you're studying: **spaced repetition**. This approach focuses on reviewing previously learned material at increasing intervals. This allows previous information to "stick" to your memory better. Here's an example of spaced repetition:

> Spaced Repetition Example
>
> You are giving a presentation in 10 days on quarterly production numbers from a team you manage. The data breaks down each team member's activities and individual results weekly and monthly.
>
> You've put the data into a presentation, and your goal is to sound comfortable and fluid, even though it's the first time you've presented it. There are also details in the tasks they performed you want to discuss in some detail.
>
> You do the entire presentation on Day 1, discussing each slide in detail, and do the same on Day 2. Day 3 is a break from it, and you do another full practice on Day 4. There's a two-day break, and you return to it on Day 7; days 5 and 6 are breaks. On Day 10, you do another walkthrough, then deliver.
>
> An important step you've already started is creating **a learning plan**. You've already outlined your goals, and you then merge your resources and timeline. That's a learning plan. Finally, break that plan into milestones, assess your progress regularly, and adjust as needed.

An important step you've already started is creating **a learning plan**. You've already outlined your goals, and you then merge your resources and timeline. That's a learning plan. Finally, break that plan into milestones, assess your progress regularly, and adjust it as needed.

An important step you've already started is creating **a learning plan**. You've already outlined your goals, and you then merge your resources and timeline. That's a learning plan. Finally, break that plan into milestones, assess your progress regularly, and adjust it as needed.

I've provided a section in the journal section of the book for you to create your learning plans. They don't have to be overwhelming, especially if you start.

Validate and Repeat

In this fast learning step, you'll test your knowledge and adjust it as you see fit. So, as you study and keep the information, you will continuously self-assess your understanding of the material. This can be done with exercises, quizzes, or flashcards to identify areas where you still have doubts.

Getting **feedback from your peers** can also be helpful. Here, you can engage in discussions, share your knowledge with others, and encourage them to ask questions.

Alternatively, you can also seek the input of an expert, where you can engage with mentors in the subject you are learning about, and they can not only test your knowledge but also correct any misunderstandings.

Be as flexible as possible in your approach. If you find specific approaches don't work, change them. Be willing to iterate and **experiment to find out what works** faster and more efficiently for you.

Determine the Level of Knowledge

Determining your knowledge might be one of the first steps before understanding something for a task. If you need practical knowledge of something to progress on a project, you might not need a deeper understanding of the subject. But it would be best if you found out your knowledge level.

Identifying the level of knowledge you need will change the approach you use. So, you need to consider the context in which the knowledge you are gaining will apply. You must also identify the balance between depth and breadth of knowledge on the subject. It would help if you understood that, sometimes, it is beneficial to have deep knowledge of a specific thing and a surface understanding of related fields.

Depending on the context, you might also need to assess the trade-off between depth of knowledge and speed of acquiring that knowledge. As you might have guessed, pursuing more profound knowledge will take longer. However, if you have limited time, focusing on retaining surface knowledge might be more beneficial for the situation.

Either way, evaluate your progress to determine if you need to go in-depth into certain aspects of the knowledge you are trying to keep. You want to optimize your efforts based on your goals.

Gap Analysis

Gap analysis is another method for assessing your current state and individual performance. It can also help you view the state of your project against your desired target. It helps identify the gap or missing knowledge between where you are and where you want to be. Gap analysis can determine the level of expertise needed and how far along you are from a knowledge goal.

This is an excellent approach if the project or the Learning is long-term. You may need to wait to do a gap analysis, but having it as a tool as you grow in your job can be really helpful.

The process is straightforward: First, determine your goals, which you have probably already achieved. Then, assess your current state, including your existing performance, processes, capabilities, and resources, so you have an accurate picture of where you are. Once that is done, you must identify the gap between where you are and where you want to be. Essentially, you are determining where the gap is.

Once you have determined the gap, look at internal and external factors to understand the reasons for the gap. You know your goals, where you are, what the gap is, and the causes of it, so you need to devise an action plan and other strategies to bridge that gap between where you are and where you want to be. Now, to bridge the gap, there are a myriad of things that you can do, but they all depend on the context.

You may need to gain new skills, implement new processes, or allocate resources. Whatever it is, it makes the gap smaller and brings you closer to the goals you want to achieve. Then, you must implement the changes outlined in your action plan and monitor your progress.

A gap analysis is a great way to realize where you are on your journey and actively bridge the gap between where you are and where you want to be. There are other benefits.

For instance, it allows you to ensure that your efforts align with your goals and help you stay on track. It is also a great way to optimize your resources by allocating them more efficiently so you can focus on the areas that need improvement.

Your performance and productivity can improve because you have highlighted areas needing growth. And, because you have based your analysis on data, you get an accurate insight that will allow you to make better-informed decisions. You can look at the GAP analysis as a strategic tool that you can use to identify and address any discrepancies between where you are currently and where you want to be.

Johari Window Concept

A helpful concept geared more toward self-awareness and interpersonal relationships can give you great personal and professional insights into your development and be a great tool to use when you start a new job. The Johari Window is a psychological model used to describe how people perceive themselves and how they are perceived.

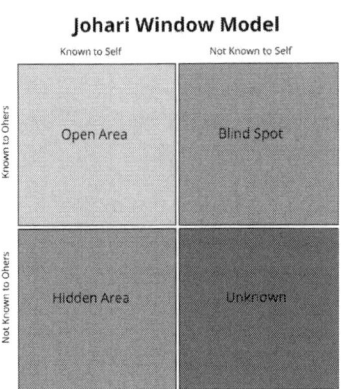

The Johari Window model has four quadrants: the open, the blind spot, the hidden, and the unknown. The open quadrant is where you have characteristics of the individual's personality and behavior. These are known to you and others, so the quadrant is called "open." The blind spot quadrant is where you add characteristics of yourself that are not known but are apparent to others. The "blind spot" quadrant is because others see it, but you don't. The hidden quadrant has information you know about you, but the others don't, mainly because you chose not to reveal it to others. These can be feelings or private thoughts you don't want to share. And last, the unknown quadrant is any personality trait that neither you nor others know, such as undiscovered emotions, potential, or talents.

The main application of this concept is for you to explore your self-awareness, figure out how others perceive you, and discover hidden characteristics you didn't know about yourself. This can improve communication, especially with interpersonal relationships, because it mitigates the blind spot quadrant and increases your knowledge of yourself. Viewing your job and working through the Johari Window can also strengthen your work by promoting openness among the team members.

How Do You Learn?

Despite how you approach your Learning, you need to identify the best way for you to learn, and here, there's no right or wrong way of doing it; you need to find out the best way to learn faster and more efficiently. There are five different common ways to learn:

1. **Visual learner:** You use images, diagrams, graphs, or any other visual aids to understand what you're studying.

2. **Auditory learner:** You learn best through listening to lectures, discussions, or verbal explanations.

3. **Kinesthetic or tactile learner:** You learn through practical application.

4. **Reading and writing learner:** You learn more efficiently through reading and writing so you can better process and internalize information.

5. **Multimodal:** You learn to use all these methods above.

Visual Learner

The characteristic of visual learners is that they process information better when a visual aid is used. There are a few strategies that I want to highlight, but if you're a visual learner, some of these techniques might work better than others. The most common one is using visual aids, as mentioned above, such as mind maps, diagrams, or infographics—anything where you can transform complex concepts into something visual.

There's also color coding, similar to the stoplight report, where you highlight the critical points of the knowledge you want to absorb to emphasize its importance and help you retain it. You don't have to stick to the stoplight colors, and you can add more depending on the context, but the simpler it is, the easier it gets. Flashcards are another form of visual Learning. Build flashcards with the visual element on one side and the explanation on the other. When studying things for the first time, before you come up with your visual aids, you can try to create mental images to represent abstract concepts as you read or listen to the material. This will make it easier for you later to come up with visual aids.

Visual Learner Example

I have a client who progressed quickly in his role at a medical services company. He was the ultimate visual learner. Before our sessions, he would send a text with a picture of the whiteboard that included an agenda, ideas, and relevant data.

His thoughts and agenda for our session were on that whiteboard. He found the visuals of a whiteboard were his way of learning and sharing his knowledge.

Auditory Learner

Listening and verbal communication are the most effective ways to learn if you're an auditory learner. You retain more information through lectures, verbal explanations, and discussions. There are a few strategies that you can use. For instance, audiobooks or even podcasts about the subject might be great ways to learn. You can also attend lectures, webinars, or even seminars if you can find some on the topic you need to know. One way to reinforce what you have learned as an auditory learner is to recite information by repeating essential information. Alternatively, you can also explain concepts to others to reinforce that knowledge.

Group discussion is also a great way to retain information and even deepen knowledge when you engage in verbal exchanges about the topic you want to keep. Either way, listen actively to whatever spoken content you are listening to and consider taking notes to highlight the main points you want to remember.

Kinesthetic or Tactile Learner

If you are a tactile or kinesthetic learner, you want hands-on experiences and practical applications. However, depending on the topic, this may be harder. Either way, here are some methods you can use. If you are this type of learner, you learn best by doing. Seek activities that involve physical engagement of the knowledge you want to keep, such as simulations or experiments. You should apply your knowledge to real-life situations to better solidify your understanding.

Using props or objects to visualize and understand abstract concepts, such as building blocks to represent mathematical equations, is a great way to add that tactile experience to certain topics. Physical movement can enhance retention, so make sure you add breaks during your study sessions. The Pomodoro Technique I'll share shortly could be helpful.

Reading and Writing Learners

If you are more of a reading and writing learner, then you retain more information by doing that: reading and writing. The best way to do this is through note-taking, especially during your study sessions or lectures. You can also do this by reading textbooks or watching a video. Summaries are also an excellent way for you to remember knowledge. After a review session, you can write a summary in your own words to help reinforce what you have just learned.

Here, you can use flashcards, too, but instead of images, you can have questions on one side and answers on the other. The simple act of writing them down and reviewing them can help you retain more information. Lastly, another technique you can use is journaling, where you record your insights, thoughts, or anything related to your study. You'll see in the Journal section of the book how you can use journaling techniques.

Multimodal Learner

Individuals who are multimodal learners are adaptable and can switch between learning methods as they see fit, depending on the different situations. You can use any of the methods I mentioned above or a combination, depending on the context and the material you are learning about.

You can use a wide array of learning resources, such as instructional videos, audiobooks, or textbooks, and can quickly switch to another method if the one you are using is not working. This understanding of what is and isn't working will make you more efficient so you can better optimize your learning process.

Understanding your dominant learning style can enhance how fast your retention of knowledge becomes. But even if you like to stick to one learning style, you should remain open to incorporating elements from other styles as you see fit.

The Pomodoro Technique

I often use the Pomodoro technique in my writing and general work, and it is an excellent method to use when you're studying to break down complex concepts into smaller ones. This technique comprises bursts of focus (between 20 and 25 minutes, but this is entirely up to you) followed by a 5 to 7-minute break. After you have completed four sessions, you take a more extended break (between 15 and 30 minutes). This technique is very adaptable, and as you use it more, you'll find that you will understand what works better for you. But let's go through the method in more detail.

There are four significant benefits or characteristics of using this technique. The first is prioritization, where the method itself encourages you to prioritize your focus on the most critical tasks. You first select the task you want to work on by listing the topics you need to learn. Then, you determine which task is most critical for you or requires your attention first. With this technique, you're solely focused on a single task during a session, increasing your productivity.

This is a great way to decrease your feeling overwhelmed because you **break complex concepts and tasks into smaller chunks**, making it easier to focus on them and ensuring that you dedicate your time and energy to the most critical task first.

The Pomodoro technique is characterized by its **timeboxing**, where you impose structured time limits on your study sessions and promote efficient Learning. Start by setting a timer (usually between 20 and 25, but it can be longer or shorter) representing a session. During that time, you focus only on the task with no interruptions. After each session, you take a quick break (5 to 7 minutes), and once you have done four sessions, you take a slightly longer break. This increases your productivity because you are more focused on what you are doing and do your work uninterrupted. It also helps prevent burnout because you are taking regular breaks.

Another benefit of the Pomodoro technique is that it **eliminates distractions**. Before beginning a session, identify potential distractions, such as phone notifications and social media. During a session, if you get distracted, make a note of it so you can eliminate it during the next break. This allows you to improve your focus by identifying and managing your distractions, which improves your ability to stay focused on the task. By minimizing distractions or interruptions, you allow deeper comprehension of the subject.

The **regular breaks** in the Pomodoro technique are vital in contributing to the fast Learning you want to achieve and reducing the chance of fatigue. These breaks allow you to restore your energy without completely losing focus because they are short and frequent, so they allow you to keep your energy levels high and your focus. As I have said, it is a great way to reduce fatigue, especially when what you need to learn is long and complex, allowing you to maintain focus for extended periods.

By implementing this technique, you can prioritize tasks, allocate the time you have to Learning, reduce interruptions or distractions, and ensure regular breaks. All of this will help you learn any subject faster while promoting a balanced study routine.

Summary

This chapter offered an action plan to acquire the knowledge needed to perform at a top level in your new role. The critical process steps were to assess and focus, study and review, validate and iterate what you've learned, and determine the knowledge level you need.

Gap analysis is a proven approach to building a learning plan. Another element of fast Learning is understanding your learning style. The most common ones are visual, auditory, kinesthetic, tactile, auditory, reading or writing, and multimodal.

Two learning tools are spaced repetition and the Pomodoro technique.

Using the models and tools in this chapter will fill in the gaps in your knowledge while still contributing to your role.

The next chapter focuses on the last of the three tracks of the Game Plan: Building Relationships. It can be the most beneficial of the three, but having tools and models, like the other Game Plan tracks, will make it more rewarding and enjoyable.

Building Relationships

Game Plan Track 3

Scenario

This new role is more visible than any role you've ever had and there are lots of teams and people you'll interact with. Your first couple weeks have been meeting after meeting with individuals and team how you'll work closely with. They will also depend on the work you'll be doing, so building a solid relationship is key.

You realize each person and group is unique, they have different communication styles, needs and quirks. It feels challenging figuring out how to best work with them, since they have different needs and approaches.

Learning to accommodate them and build strong relationships, while also focusing on the other two tracks of the Game Plan feels daunting.

The third track of the new job success model consists of building relationships. To recap, we looked at tools to help you demonstrate and deliver value and how you can become a fast learner. These are great ways to become successful at your new job, but building relationships may be more critical.

Trust is the often-forgotten foundation of relationship building, and it only happens sometimes. You have to be consistent and consider other people's needs and interests.

Methods to Build Relationships

You can build trust with your peers at a new job in many ways, but some methods work better than others. For instance, you might have heard of the 80/20 rule, which can also apply to building relationships.

In relationship building, the rule states that 80% of the conversations you have with your new peers should be about them, and only 20% should be about you. This means that you should prioritize learning about them and their needs. Now, how can you do this?

One way to implement this rule is by **actively listening** during your conversations. You show genuine interest in their work and lives by paying close attention to what your peers tell you. While doing this, you should also ask open-ended questions so there's more to discuss instead of a simple yes or no, which might end the conversation. This is a great way to establish rapport because you're **showing interest**, which builds trust and is a great way to cement a relationship's foundation. Also, by listening more, you can **gain great insights** into your peers' expertise and experiences and about themselves.

Using the 80/20 rule gives you a better chance **of learning about their challenges and aspirations.** This will help you align your contributions and efforts with their and their team's goals. Try these two different approaches.

In one-on-one conversations, you can schedule a meeting with your peers and discuss responsibilities, roles, and any other challenges they might face.

Or through a team discussion, where the team meets, understands the challenges, and **brainstorms** to gain insights into solutions or opportunities that the team might follow. This prompts collaborative solutions because you identify the challenges and collaborate on solutions that will contribute to the team's success. It shows that you will help overcome any obstacles for the sake of the team.

However, avoid **any type of gossip** and instead **ask about how your role can help them.** This is because gossip can harm not only the team's dynamics but also their relationships. By focusing on offering your support and understanding how your role can benefit them and, as a result, the team, you create trust. You can implement this through positive contributions and constructive discussions instead of gossiping, which creates negativity.

By asking your peers how you can assist them in their roles, you are offering your expertise and resources to help them achieve their goals. As I have mentioned, this builds trust and respect among your colleagues since they consider you a reliable and supportive team member.

Another thing is to pay attention to and understand **how teams and groups prefer to communicate**. By understanding how your peers like to speak, you can increase collaboration with the team. You can ask for the type of communication they prefer or observe their communication style because it might be more complex. There might be a difference among your colleagues; some prefer messaging or email, and others prefer face-to-face meetings.

As you might have guessed, this makes communication more efficient by tailoring it to your peers' preferences. It also improves relationships because you are adapting to their communication style, which shows consideration and respect.

Conversations are strongest when we speak clearly, early and often about our shared interests. Bringing people along on shared interests and the journey is worth it.
HOLLY O'DELL PRESIDENT AND CEO | MONTANA STATE FUND

Wharton professor Maurice Schweitzer and his team have introduced a practical communication framework, the **"conversational circumplex."** Despite its complex name, this model is a practical and effective tool for understanding the participants' goals in your conversations, leading to more successful interactions (Basiouny, 2022).

This framework maps conversations along two categories: **informational**, where data is shared or gathered, and **relational**, where relationships are developed or deepened.

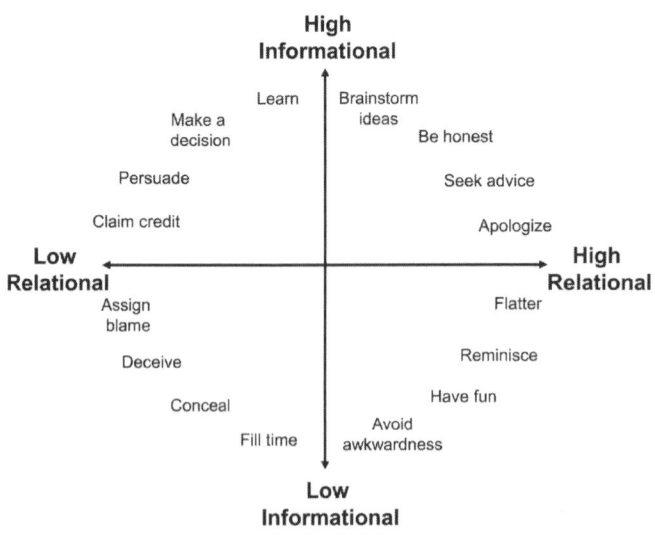

Current Opinion in Psychology

This framework tells us that precise conversation goals allow us to be more prepared, plan better, and increase our chances of success in those conversations. This framework can also apply to work-related conversations and personal conversations.

Conversational goals vary widely depending on the context and the relationships you have with the person on the other side of the conversation, so adapting strategies is crucial. In his paper, Schweitzer emphasizes that showing commitment to a relationship is vital, regardless of the context. The research by Schweitzer and his colleagues found that when people pursue multiple conversational goals, their chances of success increase when these goals are more similar.

For example, according to the circumplex shown in the study, brainstorming ideas are far more compatible than "being honest" and "concealing information," which are opposites in that graph. The study identifies specific behaviors that might arise from conflicting goals.

For instance, backhanded compliments or humble bragging should be able to be identified, assessed, and compared to your goals. The authors suggest using the circumplex to help you plan the conversation's goals and, after the conversation, evaluate what you have achieved.

One last thing is **setting follow-up actions** and meetings. When you effectively follow up, you show your commitment and accountability in building and supporting relationships. After meetings, or even better, at the close of a conference (before people move on to something else), you want a simple action plan with bullet points and deadlines to ensure that the different responsibilities and who does what are clearly understood.

Also, by scheduling follow-up meetings (either you directly or a team member), you can review the progress of specific projects, discuss any challenges, and make adjustments as you see fit. The two significant benefits of this are accountability and reliability. By following through on your commitments and scheduling follow-up meetings, you show your accountability and reliability. This also promotes continuous improvement, ensuring that relationships and collaborations continue to develop positively.

Building Relationships by Asking Questions

Let's start by providing some questions you can use. I've discussed some of these earlier, but let's go a little deeper, starting with **"What triggered you to join?"**

This question encourages your colleagues to share their personal and professional sides. You can follow up with questions about what aspects of the company attracted them the most and made them decide to join or what they expect in the future. By asking these questions, you show curiosity and genuine interest in understanding their motivations. You are also appealing for emotional engagement by asking about a personal connection they might have to the role or the company.

By asking, **"What are the challenges and opportunities your group currently faces?"** You are asking about any specific challenges or opportunities within their team. For instance, you can learn about recent situations or projects to understand current challenges better. It would help if you encouraged them to provide recent examples of their work and even discuss potential solutions or strategies that they can use related to the challenges they've mentioned. This also expresses concern and a willingness to collaborate and contribute to addressing such challenges.

Now, you can also get a little more personal but still ask a question related to work, such as, **"What has your team done that makes you the proudest?"** Here, you are inviting them to share a particular team achievement and trying to understand its impact. Besides encouraging your peers to celebrate their team's success, you also explore how collaboration and team effort work and contribute to the team's success.

If you ask, **"How do you see my role in helping you and the team?"** you seek to understand your colleague's expectations and potential collaboration with your role. You can ask them about projects or tasks where they believe your expertise might be helpful. This highlights your interest in working collaboratively and contributing to the company's shared goals. You're also understanding where your role aligns with theirs, and you clearly understand how your skills can benefit them.

One last example of a question from which you can gain more insight is **"What's the best way to communicate?"** When you ask this question, you are expressing your willingness to adapt to their communication style. You're also ensuring you can communicate with them effectively and with a more robust mutual understanding.

While the questions above are a great start, you might need more and have to come up with your own questions, too. For that, make sure that your questions give you some insights or help. You already know you should avoid yes-or-no questions because they don't encourage a deeper conversation. However, it would help to let the other person share an accomplishment or a win.

With your line of questioning, try to find areas of alignment, such as identifying common goals, interests, or challenges so that you can connect with your colleagues. And always try to pose questions that move the conversation forward.

Developing Small Talk as a Skill

Small talk is a vital skill that helps build rapport, encourage connections, and create a safe social atmosphere. We've covered some, and I'll reinforce them and add additional approaches.

It would help if you always started **with a greeting,** such as "Hello" or Good to see you." This sets a positive tone and energy level for the conversation that follows. Remember to ask open-ended questions to encourage discussion and actively listen when you're talking with your colleagues.

Try to **find some common ground**; a great way to do this is through **shared experiences**. This could be anything, from an event you both attended to recent news or vacation topics. However, **avoid contro-**

versial issues, such as religion or politics, at least when building trust with your new colleagues. You can **use compliments but be measured**; exaggerating might appear fake. When you feel it is appropriate, you can transition from small talk to topics that interest you more.

You can go deeper to find common ground since it's a great way to connect with someone. I would like to ask about their hobbies and other interests they might have. Questions like, **"Do you have any pastimes or hobbies?"** or **"What do you enjoy doing in your free time?"** These are good questions to ask if you have anything in common. You can also ask about their **favorite books, movies, or music.** If you have similar tastes, you can recommend some of your favorites to them.

Exploring experiences is also a great way to find common ground. For instance, you can **talk about traveling** or places they've lived. Similarly, you can ask about sports or activities they like to do.

While you try to build connections with your new colleagues, it is crucial that you also **share some personal aspects about yourself**. Here, you can share any aspirations you have, such as those for your family or any commitment to personal growth you have detailed for yourself. Sharing personal stories or anecdotes that relate to the topic you are talking about can be a great way to connect with other people because they usually provide insights into your personality and experiences.

For instance, any milestones worth sharing, such as **reaching a career goal** or **personal achievement**. When the time is right and appropriate, you can also express vulnerability. You can talk about challenges or how you have overcome some of them. This is important because vulnerability can deepen your connection with others.

One of the most important things you should know is **the pace and depth of that personal sharing**. This should always align with your intimacy level with that colleague. If you're getting to know them in professional settings, focus only on light personal areas. You can explore more personal topics when you finally build confidence with them in a more casual setting. As I have said, small talk is an art, and it takes some time to master, but it is a great way to build connections with others.

> Example: Small Talk as a Skill
>
> An organization hired me to coach one of their leaders. The leader struggled to connect and bond with the team he had been newly promoted to manage. He was quite shy, which made communication stilted and awkward.
>
> We created a plan for him to learn to reach out in stages. The plan revolved around techniques to break the ice and create a more comfortable environment within the team.
>
> I guided him to initiate conversations with his team members, starting with small and **safe topics such as food or travel**. This seemingly simple approach proved to be a comfortable way for him to connect with his team on a more personal level. His commitment and effort were commendable.
>
> Over time, he overcame the initial hurdles, leading to improved communication and relationships. He was able to delve deeper into his team's dynamics with ease.

The Four Constituent Organizational Graph

While there are many organizational graphs, this one will help drive your career success. It prioritizes crucial relationships within the organization. These four constituents are your leadership team, peers, team (if you are a leader), and customers. Building relationships with each constituent and building trust is imperative. Let's break each one down.

Leadership Team

As you know, the relationship you cultivate with your leaders is the bedrock of your professional journey. It's not just about giving them regular updates on your work; it's about creating a plan to do so. Share your challenges, achievements, and seek their guidance to align your goals with those of the organization. This process builds trust, a currency that can lead to career advancements, mentorship, and a plethora of other opportunities. It's a tangible demonstration of your commitment to the company's objectives.

Peers

Collaboration within your team is not just a nice-to-have, it's a necessity. Actively seek opportunities to work with your colleagues, share knowledge, and offer help. This isn't just about building a positive relationship, it's about fostering a culture of teamwork and collaboration. The benefits are manifold-it enhances problem-solving, sparks creativity, and ultimately, contributes to a more productive and harmonious work environment.

Your Team

This is for readers who are leaders, but even if you're not one, understanding the concepts helps. As a leader, you must prioritize your team's progress, career growth, and well-being. For this to happen, give them regular feedback, create clear expectations, and give them opportunities to grow. If you do that, you will develop excellent leadership skills essential to building a great team and for your own career.

Customers

In this last section, identify the customer's needs and problems so you can deliver excellent service and build long-term relationships with them. As you know, satisfied customers lead to business growth, referrals, or repeat business. So, by serving customers well, you are also showing a commitment to the business's growth.

These are groups you serve and answer to in the work you do. So, your title and experience don't matter less than how you work with them. Develop an action plan for each constituent, then monitor and iterate. You need to know your progress with each constituent and understand if you are meeting your action plans and goals. Getting good at mastering your relationships with these teams is extremely important. For instance, a strong relationship with your leadership team can open the doors to many opportunities, just as significant interactions with your peers can create a supportive work environment.

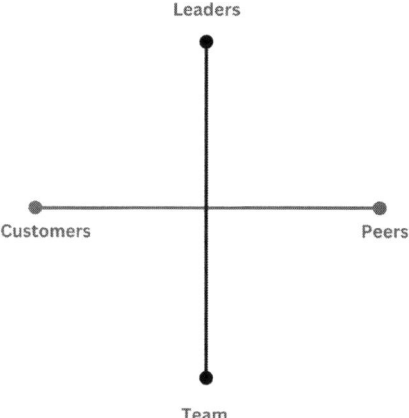

Your 4 Constituents

By developing action plans for each of these four groups, monitoring your progress, and mastering every one of these constituents, you can improve your career and help your organization grow.

How Well Do You Know Your Constituents?

Four questions about the different groups are important to answer, and I'm going to divide this section by each question and point out how you can answer it or what the goal should be for the different groups.

What Do They Need and Expect From You?

When you pose this question, looking at the leadership team, they often need a transparent and data-driven answer about the goals. Other expectations include timely updates and accountability.

Your peers often need collaboration and the sharing of knowledge when working on projects. Communication must be clear, and you must contribute to the common goals. If you are the leader, your team needs leadership and opportunities to grow. They expect regular feedback and explicit instructions.

The customers need quality, attentiveness, and solutions to their problems. Their expectations might vary, but prompt responses, consistency, and personalized service are often common expectations from them.

What Motivates Them?

Your leadership team's motivations usually revolve around achieving success through the company or meeting targets set. Opportunities to contribute with their expertise and collaboration might motivate your peers.

As a leader, the opportunity to grow and affect the organization usually motivates your team. Customers' motivation often centers on solving their problems or improving their businesses.

What Are Their Key Goals and Aspirations?

The leadership team's goals and aspirations revolve around KPIs or organizational growth targets. You can achieve that by aligning your work with the company's goals. Your peers' aspirations are a little harder to decipher, requiring effort to get to know them better. For your customers, find out their business goals and the challenges they face when using your company's services or products.

What Is Their Communication Style?

Communication style can be very different depending on the group we are talking about, and often, you have to be able to dig this out. However, it is common for the leadership team to prefer data-driven reports, and you need to adapt your communication style to align with their preferences. Your peers' communication preferences are also something that you have to uncover and build on. You need to identify the best communication channels to use, but ultimately, seek quick and open responses regardless of the type of channel you prefer.

As a leader and individual contributor, the action is the same: try to understand their preferred communication channels and attempt to meet those preferences. You can gather their choices via feedback but customize your communication accordingly. Your company established a few detailed communication channels to contact customers. However, knowing which established channels they prefer is up to you. But like most communication, you need to prioritize responsiveness and clear messages.

Explore these four questions for each group and continue to seek feedback so you can improve on them. By understanding their needs, goals, motivations, and communication styles, you can establish a better relationship with them.

Finally, being present and engaged when communicating is a simple action that almost always creates a positive experience.

Summary

Of all the Game Plan Tracks, relationship building has the most immediate rewards and potential pitfalls. The core is to build trust through being accountable and following through on all your commitments to others.

You can use several models and approaches to make relationship-building more authentic and rewarding. Active listening and using open-ended questions to learn more about the other person are foundational.

Learning how and when to use small talk is also helpful and is a straightforward way to connect.

An important relationship-building model to consider is Conversational Circumplex, which focuses on the relationship between communication and relationships. It shows how discussing different topics can grow or maintain a relationship. Using this model can help plan better interactions with key teams and individuals.

Finally, at a higher level, the Four Constituent Model can help you map out relationship building with your leaders, peers, team (if you are managing), and customers. Each is a unique group and may require different approaches to connecting and deepening your relationships.

Executing the Game Plan can be consuming in the early days of your new role. Remembering to give them equal weight regarding action taken and effort requires balance. However, the Game Plan framework provides the baseline to establish yourself in the first few months of your new role.

The next part of the book looks at the common challenges you'll face and how you can take steps to address them. Let's next look at the Five Challenges.

THE 5 CHALLENGES

 SUCCESS

 FAILURE

 CONFLICT

 AMBIGUITY

 PRIORITIZATION & NEGOTIATION

NEW JOB SUCCESS

The 5 Challenges Overview

When you start a new job, there are universal challenges everyone faces. They are so frequent they often become the subject of interview questions. Those "tell me about a time" interview questions seek to understand how you deal with these all-too-common situations.

I'll briefly introduce these challenges and dive into them more fully in subsequent chapters.

I built these five chapters based on the job search side of my coaching practice. For the book The Job Search Manifesto, I conducted a half-year survey with clients on the type of questions they were asked. It didn't take long to see a pattern.

Behavioral interview questions focus on five areas. As a long-time recruiter and coach, I understand why. We asked these questions because we knew an employee would face some or all of them, and we wanted to learn how they would deal with them during the interview process.

As my practice grew and I worked long-term with clients, they faced these. Much of my executive coaching deals with these situations.

Addressing some of these may be an uncomfortable stretch. However, the more you develop methods and models to address them, the more confidence you can have in your work.

The five most common challenges when starting a new job are **success, failure, dealing with conflict, ambiguity, prioritization, and scaling.**

The challenge of success in a new job often comes from the pressure we place on ourselves to perform well, to be seen as an asset, and to meet expectations that might come from ourselves or leadership. It often involves adapting to new workflows, dynamics of the team, or responsibilities.

Failure or the fear of failure is a different story. It often arises when you enter a new environment that you know nothing about and have to do tasks and take on responsibilities that you are not familiar with. This fear of failure often comes from making mistakes or not performing as you think you should.

Conflict often arises because of differences in communication styles, working methods, or expectations between team members. These differences, coupled with a brand-new environment, often create conflicts.

Ambiguity often emerges when your new responsibilities are unclear because you didn't understand them. This leads to uncertainty about your goals and what's expected of you.

Last, prioritization and scaling often happen when juggling different tasks, projects, or responsibilities while trying to understand which one you should prioritize first. This frequently leads to scaling issues where you must scale to meet your growing demands and responsibilities. Still, it would help if you determined your priorities to avoid becoming a challenge on its own.

Origin of These Challenges

Many of these challenges stem from everyday situations. For instance, challenges related to success or failure often come from the steep learning curve linked to a new job. These might be because of needing help adapting to new organizational cultures or technologies. Dealing with conflicts comes from differences in communication styles or expectations and a clash of distinct personalities.

It can also take some time to adapt, and it does not matter if it is a brand-new job in a different company, team, or environment. While this can be very exciting, it can also challenge you professionally and personally. This is especially true if you are new to the organization.

Despite the challenges, we can choose to see them as valuable opportunities for professional and personal growth as we adapt to them, learn from them, and develop new strategies to manage and deal with them.

The five challenges will arise throughout your working life, so building strategies to address them will keep you on track.

But the challenges may knock you off stride professionally, which can filter into your personal life. Here are some thoughts about that.

Monitoring the Balancing Act

While trying to balance our personal lives and work is always something that many struggle with, this challenge becomes more pronounced when you start a new job. Then, you are much more likely to face new and steep learning curves. You need to understand how the processes work, the company's culture, and how devices and other technologies work, for instance. It can feel like a lot and make it hard for you to disconnect from work.

You might also feel that when you start a new job, you want to show your commitment by working longer hours to prove your competence. As you give more time to your new job, you're leaving less time for your personal life, which can become a problem in itself. The uncertainty and stress of the new job can affect your personal life, too, making it harder to leave your work behind when you leave the office.

Setting boundaries between your personal life and work should be fundamental, but it can be challenging. Especially if, by setting those boundaries, you might seem disengaged with your work. Also, as with almost everyone starting a new job, you might have aspirations that prompt you to prioritize your work over your personal life to achieve those objectives, which prompts this imbalance between work and personal life.

There may also be some **peer pressure** that might affect that balance. This might not even be direct, but if they work long hours, you might feel the need to do so as well, which influences your work habits.

However, if this imbalance persists, negative consequences will show up. The most common one is issues in your relationships with your family or friends because you spend less focused time with them. This can have severe consequences, such as feeling isolated or completely disconnected from those you love. If it continues, it can even have health consequences, such as prolonged exposure to anxiety and stress, which are known triggers for illness.

It is important to highlight that all of this will affect your work life because, as humans, we strive to have balance. Now, what can you do? **Time management** is a core function; effectively using these techniques to allocate time for both your personal and work life will allow you to allocate time and energy appropriately.

However, you don't have to do this alone. Seeking **support** from friends, family, coaches, or mentors who can **offer support and advice** is a great way to find the right balance in your life. But as with everything, you should also regularly reflect on this balance to know you're moving in the right direction.

Keep in mind that **this is an ongoing process**. You might go backward occasionally, but it's essential to find the right balance consistently.

Understanding and identifying the challenge is the first step; from there, you can take steps to address those issues and maintain an overall sense of satisfaction in your personal and professional lives.

The Balancing Act is so important that the last chapter looks even more deeply at this.

Let's look at the five challenges, starting with success.

Success

Challenge 1

Scenario

When you joined the new team, you were put on a project that was moving quickly but was unstructured. You didn't have a deep understanding of all the components, so you agreed with your leader to focus on getting things better tracked and organized.

They were small but essential steps and the team quickly responded. The project came in a little ahead of schedule, but more importantly the results were better than expected.

You received a lot of praise from all levels of the organization, which felt great but created a little anxiety. Were you just lucky, in the right place at the right time?

What would people expect from you going forward; would you meet those standards?

Early success is crucial as a new staff member because it can set the pace for how others see you in the company and provide a foundation to build your career. The flip side is you can feel much of what the scenario above describes. There are a few areas to be aware of and focus on as you work on dealing with success.

Dealing with success is not all about your accomplishments; it is also about how you integrate your successes into your work.

How to Integrate Early Success

As you might have guessed, embracing continuous learning is essential. Early success in your new company or role often comes from initial bursts of enthusiasm and the latest expertise and skills you bring with you. But it would help if you recognized that you can't stop there; more work must be done.

Many rely on this early success and just let things go. Still, there's a lesson to be learned here where you can continue to seek opportunities to learn from your experiences, regardless of whether they push you forward or temporarily backtrack. To continue with success, you need to seek knowledge and learn from the experiences you have along the way.

Don't view your early success as a standalone event; try to connect it to bigger goals and what the company wants. It would help to see this success as a building block for something more you can link to the company's vision. Of course, for that to happen, you need to have a clear picture of the company's values and objectives.

One last thing: as you gain knowledge, remember that knowledge should be shared with the rest of your team. This way, you are helping the team and the organization, too.

Dealing With Praise and Recognizing Others

Don't treat receiving praise or compliments as just gratification. Don't get me wrong; it should be, but you can also consider it a challenge. As a new employee, you need to know how to navigate this with **humility** and not let it go to your head.

When receiving praise, the first thing to do is to accept it graciously and maintain a humble but positive attitude. A simple but sincere "thank you" is often enough. You can also express a little more gratitude: Instead of just saying "thank you," you can say, "Thank you for the recognition," or "I wouldn't have done it without you."

It is essential to reflect on the praise you received and understand the actions that led to that recognition. This will allow you to understand your strengths and what other areas you can work on. Consider how you share credit because this shows humility and deepens relationships.

Success is rarely achieved alone, and when you work in an organization, this success is often linked to your team, so you openly share the credit with them.

Remain humble instead of boastful. Remember that humility is something people admire, and you want to maintain a positive relationship with the rest of your team.

It is also vital that you **recognize the contribution of others** when the time is right. It would help if you did this regularly instead of waiting for some formal event to express your appreciation.

When recognizing others, be consistent and specific about what you are showing your appreciation for. Talk about the catalysts, the results, or the qualities they used to achieve the results. The more specific you are, the more it reinforces positive behaviors.

If appropriate, **recognize your peers in public**. Share their achievements in a team meeting, in emails where others are involved, or any other communication channels you use. Public recognition of their achievements boosts motivation, morale, and relationships.

Also, celebrate milestones with your colleagues, anything from their achievements to the success of a project. Praise your colleagues when they deserve it, but also promote a culture where every colleague acknowledges and praises each other. This can make working together really enjoyable.

Try this by leading by example. In fact, as a new team member, this might be even more effective because sometimes others are more receptive to new things when people from outside the company or that they don't know that well do them.

Also, always ensure that the praise and recognition you give are **equitable and inclusive**. Recognize unique contributions to ensure that every colleague is valued.

Recognition does not mean praising all the time. **Giving helpful, balanced feedback** can be a significant form of recognition. When you offer feedback to your colleagues, you are not only recognizing their efforts but also helping them improve.

Dealing with praise and recognizing others promotes a positive and supportive work culture in the workplace. Among its many benefits, it can enhance job satisfaction and foster teamwork. Positive praise is a great way to build strong professional relationships in the work environment.

Impostor Syndrome

A pervasive new job challenge related to early success is impostor syndrome. This widely-known challenge occurs when **people doubt their abilities** and achievements and feel like they **don't deserve the success they have**. Another symptom of this syndrome is the fear of being **exposed as a fraud**, even if they have clear evidence of being competent at what they do.

While this early success can undoubtedly boost your confidence and even validate your capabilities, it can trigger impostor syndrome because you might question whether you earned that success or if it was just luck. Imposter Syndrome was a vital part of this chapter's opening scenario.

When impostor syndrome is associated with early success, there are a few common triggers to watch for. For instance, reaching success early in your career can set high expectations for the rest of your job, and from that moment on, you might feel mounting pressure to either maintain or even exceed the level of success you have had, which often leads to self-doubt. As I have said, attributing success to luck can trigger this syndrome, and this does not mean "luck" in the traditional sense, but attributing your success to external factors like timing.

Another trigger is **comparisons with colleagues** who have had different career trajectories. Comparing yourself to others and doubting your abilities is an all-too-common attribute of imposter syndrome.

Some signs that show you are struggling with impostor syndrome include feeling like a fraud, regardless of evidence that says otherwise. Also downplaying your achievements or attributing them to luck, trying to seek approval from others at all times, avoiding situations where you think you'll be exposed as a fraud, or even overworking to compensate for feelings that you are not good enough.

Of course, we might feel like that sometimes; after all, we all doubt ourselves. However, it is essential that once you see some of those signs, you adopt strategies to overcome them. The first step is to acknowledge and accept it. Impostor syndrome is widespread, and many successful people have experienced it in their careers. Accepting it is just part of the process of overcoming it. Ty and refocus on your achievements. Write your successes, and when self-doubt hits, review them to remind yourself of your wins.

Push aside or distract yourself from negative self-talk. Focus on realistic, positive thoughts and be compassionate with yourself. The journal at the end of the book offers you a place to capture this.

If you can't keep those thoughts away and feel more like an impostor, then it is time to seek help. You don't have to go to formal therapy; sometimes, talking to friends, colleagues, or a coach can help you understand your skills. Therapy can be an option for taking the initial steps that don't help reduce imposter syndrome anxiety.

One last thing about overcoming impostor syndrome is to set realistic expectations and understand that **everybody has setbacks** or failures throughout their careers. Still, by **setting realistic expectations**, you know that to grow, sometimes you need to fail.

Another fear that might grow during these circumstances is the fear of **not being able to replicate early success**. This links to the pressure of expectations we've seen with impostor syndrome, but sometimes you have this fear without having impostor syndrome, and many differences go into this. For instance, the fear of falling short of expectations might completely stop you from pursuing new challenges.

Many of the strategies used to overcome impostor syndrome work with the fear of not being able to replicate the early success you have had, but there are other solutions that you can try in this case. For instance, **practicing mindfulness** is one of those methods. Interrupting negative thinking, even for a few minutes, is a proven method to reduce their impact.

Summary

Accomplishments by themselves are the starting point. Your success grows when you **integrate, learn, and contribute** positively to your company.

As we've also seen previously, **part of becoming successful is building relationships** with everyone who works with you and communicating effectively with your colleagues and leaders.

Other things that contribute to your success include being **adaptable to different situations**. The workplace is dynamic; responding to changes is vital there. This is especially true post-pandemic when where we work and how often we are back in the office are constantly developing.

Career growth is intrinsically linked to **developing your problem-solving skills**. Try to approach every problem with a problem-solving mindset. When faced with a challenge, analyzing the issue and its causes so you can come up with creative solutions is also part of being adaptable.

You should also be **receptive to change** and grow as the circumstances do. Being resilient in the face of unexpected developments is part of it. Remember that failures happen, but you should use them as an opportunity to grow and improve instead of letting them be something you worry too much about. We'll touch on that in the next chapter.

You also want to work on effective time management to achieve success. This includes prioritizing your responsibilities and tasks to ensure your focus is on the activities that affect your achievement the most. The Pomodoro technique, which we've discussed before, is an excellent method for prioritizing your activities. **Multitasking often reduces productivity**, and you should avoid it. Focus on one task at a time and finish it before moving on to the next one.

Networking actively can help you succeed, both within and outside your company. You're expected to build relationships with your colleagues, mentors, and others in the industry. I have mentioned this before, but attending meetups, conferences, and events is a great way to network. Your connections can provide great insights and opportunities throughout your career.

Showing leadership, regardless of your title at your company, can be a great way to establish a path to success. This is accomplished by taking the initiative and contributing to the success of the business and your colleagues. Again, leading by example is a great way to show just that by showing others your work ethic, resilience, or accountability.

However, I have again highlighted your **work-life balance**. You ensure that your well-being is also a priority. So, allocating some time for hobbies, spending time with family and friends, and even relaxing will contribute as much to your success as actively working for the company.

Also, **avoid overcommitting** or taking on too much work by learning to say no when you simply can't do more. This will help you prevent burnout, one of the significant causes of failure.

You need to incorporate early successes into your continued work occasionally. It is an ongoing process, so you must continuously work on it. Ultimately, building on success in a planned and focused way is an outstanding model for continuing success.

Failure

Challenge 2

Scenario

Given an immediate task when you first joined a new team, you're told this has been a challenge for the team to deliver consistent results. Undaunted you dive in, only to find there have been multiple direction changes in the approach and delivery – nothing ever worked.

You try yet another approach and get very little feedback. And the feedback you do get is unclear and negative. After several attempts to adapt to feedback, your leader says another team will take on the task and removes you from it.

Your immediate response is to feel both shame and failure. You may also start to question your skills and competence. You wonder if you can recover from this in the eyes of your boss and team.

Failure is the mirror of success, with many of us seeing failure as a situation that will tear down our careers. It can slow down or sidetrack a career for a time, but you can mitigate failure. Looking at a failure through a lens of doom or worst case is corrosive and often self-fulfilling.

There is a famous (often overused) statement in tech: "Fail Fast." The core idea is to learn from your mistakes and incorporate them into your next round of work. This approach requires resilience and self-forgiveness. But failure can ultimately be a strong, positive career event.

Incorporating Lessons Learned

A lot of my coaching around failure in a career is to remind clients failure is an outstanding teacher. However, learning from the lessons requires seeing it as an opportunity to grow. Incorporating lessons based on failure into your future work is a proven model. It's the core of the "failing fast" approach.

The first step is reflection. You can't learn anything unless you reflect on it, understand where it comes from, and consider what you can do differently next time.

After experiencing a setback:

1. Take your time to understand the things that went wrong.

2. Analyze what happened and decide what you could have done differently to avoid that failure.

3. Be as honest as you can if you want to overcome that challenge the next time you face it.

Once you've reflected on it, gather and collate the main lessons. What are the lessons you have gained from failing? There's always something to learn after you fail. Here are some coaching questions I often ask:

- What did you learn about yourself, especially about how you responded?

- How would you change the approach you chose?

- What early problems did you dismiss or ignore?

- How would you better communicate both the status and your concerns?

- How would you better incorporate real-time feedback into your work?

Answering these questions can give great insights into avoiding repeating the same mistakes you made.

When you fail at something, you must understand how to apply the lessons learned to adjust your strategy and approach and make better decisions. With this, you will come up with new methods based on the experiences you have had.

Feedback is another excellent way to improve after failure. Whether from colleagues, coaches, or leaders, seek perspectives on overcoming some of your challenges.

For example, I encourage clients to journal and write about their successes and what they learned from failure.

You can do something similar and use it as a reference point for when you must decide and are in a similar position, as well as a reminder of your progress so far. To make that easier, I've included a journal with this book to help you document these lessons.

Avoid Throwing Others Under the Bus

When you face failure in the workplace, you must try to stay professional. **You can't blame others**, even if they share some fault for the failure. You can be more honest in private with that person, but public critiques are a sure way to be ostracized and no longer trusted. Watching your emotions is important. When you feel emotions creeping in, make sure you pause before responding. Give yourself that extra moment to consider what you say.

Processing failure, publicly and privately, starts by **taking responsibility for your actions**. Responsibility leads to accountability.

Second, **look for solutions** instead of looking for someone to blame. This is also true if someone is trying to blame you. Shift the conversation toward the problem and attempt to find the solution constructively. Also, if you point fingers at others or take offense when others do the same to you, it begins a broken relationship with your colleagues. Getting into a cycle of accusations can quickly escalate to damaging trust and relationships.

When facing failure, avoid the word "you" and instead use the word "I" or "we" if you are working as a team. This is an essential aspect of shifting the conversation from placing the blame on others.

Also, if you have to talk with someone about failure, make sure you do it in a private setting instead of addressing the issue in public, as the latter might be perceived as shaming.

Now, when one of your colleagues has made a mistake where you have no part to blame, always **offer your support** and ask if there's anything you can do to assist them in coming up with a solution. Don't offer harsh criticism because we all make mistakes from time to time. Next time, it can be you, and I'm sure you'd prefer someone supporting you instead of blaming or criticizing you.

When you offer support, try to put yourself in their shoes and understand their perspective. This viewpoint makes it easier for them to explain the situation and help them develop a solution.

These are just some practices you can follow to create a more inclusive and collaborative environment where your colleagues feel encouraged to take responsibility for their actions. But you have to lead by example here and do the same thing so you can all look for solutions together instead of pointing fingers at one another.

Self-Motivation After Failure

When you face failure, you might feel demotivated to carry on the excellent work you have been doing. However, you must stay resilient and try to motivate yourself. Let's talk about some methods you can use for self-motivation after failure or setbacks.

Maintaining a growth mindset is important because it encourages you to believe that your setbacks and failures are opportunities to learn. Sometimes, **setting new goals** after you have failed at something might be a good idea. Make sure the goals you set are achievable so you can regain your confidence and motivation.

One thing many of my clients do in coaching is to re-visualize success and remind themselves of their long-term goals. I've seen this help many clients rekindle the determination and motivation they need to continue.

Summary

Here are the sound coaching ideas I would like to share with clients to help them deal with failure. One of them is maintaining their perspective. This means keeping your failures in perspective by understanding that they are part of your long-term success.

Monitoring your reaction is essential. You may perceive a situation as dire when the rest of the organization is much less concerned. It can often be hard to be impartial when your actions are being evaluated.

Failures don't define you unless you let them. The one area you control is your response to the situation. That is a core principle of coaching and personal growth.

Stay adaptable. After we fail, we question and possibly lose faith in our skills and knowledge. However, being flexible and adaptable to any circumstance are skills to grow and nurture, not avoid. An agile approach allows you to pivot faster in response to any challenge that might come your way.

Maintaining and growing a supportive network around you might help you keep up with your work and not let failure get in your head. This means colleagues, friends, coaches, or anyone you trust and want guidance and encouragement from when times are rough.

I want to highlight a final idea: when facing failure, remember **your "why."** This means keeping in mind the reasons you pursued your career and why the goals you want to achieve are important. The why provides all the motivation you need to get out of that slump and continue to pursue the things you have set out to do.

Failure is never a dead end, but not pursuing what you want because of failure certainly is. Incorporate failure lessons, maintain professionalism, and stay motivated for success. Resilience in the face of failure is the only way to grow and progress.

Dealing with Conflict

Challenge 3

Scenario

You are given a project that in an area you have wanted to work on for months. It was a key reason you took this role and you are excited to make a solid contribution.

When you present your ideas and action plan, a key member of your team shoots it down fast and hard. It was a brutal, public critique you didn't expect and weren't ready for. When you talk to your leader, they say, "That's just the way that other person talks; don't worry about it." But that's easier said than done, especially when the comments continue.

You see value in the other party's comments but the tone and negativity is really hard to process. Every time you are in a meeting with that person, you choke up and struggle to communicate. This only makes the situation worse.

Talking with the other person seems to be the only way forward, but taking the first step, or any step feels beyond your ability.

Conflict can be a loaded word, often triggering worry and avoidance. But it's usually a catalyst for individual and organizational growth. Ideally, conflict sits at the midpoint between a debate and a heated argument.

Whatever the level of disagreement, using tools and methods to move from conflict to cooperation is essential to your job and career success. This is a key focus as a coach: helping clients (at every level, individual contributors to leaders) deal with debate, disagreements, and conflicts. And every model of **conflict resolution begins with communication.**

In the earlier chapter on Relationship Building in the Game Plan section, I shared three core communication techniques and conflict management tools: crucial conversations, radical honesty, and nonviolent communications. Each method provides a conflict management framework with powerful elements and approaches. The choice of what you use comes down to what fits you best and the situation you are dealing with.

First, here's a quick refresher on these three models. While this might initially be uncomfortable, these processes and frameworks help mitigate those feelings.

Remember that your choice of model is personal. Understand the circumstances and specific needs so you can choose the best way to deal with the conflict.

Crucial conversations provide a robust, easy-to-implement model for handling high-stakes discussions and resolving issues. The focus is on building mutual understanding and agreement, making the framework suitable for navigating critical decisions. It's a solid tool to work on specific situations.

Radical Candor is broader and best suited for creating a work environment encouraging openness and growth. It emphasizes direct and honest feedback while maintaining a caring and supportive environment.

Finally, nonviolent communication fosters empathy and understanding within diverse teams. Its focus on active listening can help defuse the tension around conflict.

Let's use these approaches more specifically to resolve conflicts.

Crucial Conversations

As I have said, the crucial conversations framework helps you navigate high-stakes and potentially conflict-ridden conversations effectively. It makes you understand that in many situations, opinions can vary, emotions can run high, and the outcomes are essential. This framework also provides you with tools and methods to ensure open and constructive dialogue through conversations.

When you start conversations with this framework, you must recognize **your motives and focus on what matters.** Crucial conversations keep you focused on what you want to achieve with the Conversation. You begin with clarity on purpose and intention, which helps you develop constructive and focused communication. However, this requires you to monitor and control your emotional responses.

Getting worked up in specific emotional conversations is easy, but you must remain in control. Creating a shared understanding by **looking at both parties' perspectives** encourages active listening, empathy, and the exploration of different perspectives to find common ground.

Essential points from a crucial conversation are **mutual purpose**, so you can establish shared goals for the Conversation and express **your views without attacking** or accusing the other person. For this, active listening is crucial, and **moving to action** means deciding on the next steps and commitments. It also means that both parties must be clear on the decisions.

This communication framework has many benefits, such as improving the ability to address and resolve conflicts constructively, improving communication skills by having difficult conversations, **increasing collaboration and decision-making** in high-stakes situations, and strengthening relationships through **empathetic and open dialogue**.

Crucial Conversation is a great communication framework for anyone looking to improve their communication skills, significantly when emotions are high, and outcomes are important.

Radical Candor

Many clients also favor radical Candor for tackling work debates, disagreements, and conflicts. This framework can also be a leadership model, but it works just as well for anyone at any level.

Think of it as a complete approach encompassing conflict management and relationship building. This is one of its key concepts. Candor's radical framework, at its core, is the belief that **solid professional relationships are built on trust.** Radical Candor encourages getting to know your colleagues personally and showing genuine interest in them. This sets the stage for more open communication.

The radical candor framework emphasizes the need to challenge others directly but constructively. This often means **providing clear and direct feedback**, even if you have to criticize. Remember that this is all about helping others. But it's shared collaboratively, making **achieving results a collective effort**. Working together and leveraging your colleagues' strengths and your own creates a clear path to success.

Like crucial conversations, radical Candor emphasizes **clear and direct feedback**, kind and clear criticism, and **active listening**.

Another idea is radical Candor: separating debate from decision-making. This approach helps ensure that **everyone's perspective is heard**. You want to take your time with decisions, which might lead to suboptimal outcomes. Essentially, this framework looks at all relevant information and points of view before deciding.

Radical Candor recognizes the critical **interplay between solid communication and strong, trust-based relationships**. Acting with this focus increases the team's and your growth.

Nonviolent Communication (NVC)

With nonviolent communication or NVC, you are trying to foster empathy, compassion, and understanding of interactions. It offers a structured approach to expressing yourself authentically and listening empathetically, which is true in situations where many perspectives need to be considered.

A foundation principle of NVC is listening empathetically: actively listening **to others' feelings and needs without judging**. Because there's no judgment, there shouldn't be verbal blaming or language that criticizes. Instead, you encourage others to express themselves in a nonjudgmental way.

Expressing gratitude and thanks is another cornerstone of the NVC framework, where you understand and express gratitude for actions from others that have contributed to your or the team's well-being. This can foster positive interactions and appreciation between the team and its members.

Let's quickly go through the main ideas behind the NVC framework.

Observation without evaluation: where you listen without criticizing or even adding any judgment or thoughts of interpretation. Here, the goal is to become more focused when communicating.

"Feelings vs. Thoughts" is tied to authentic expression in NVC. It involves distinguishing between genuine feelings and thoughts. Each brings its interpretation, and understanding each is important. This allows you to identify and express your experiences more accurately.

Another key idea of the NVC framework is expressing needs by identifying and communicating unmet needs that trigger particular feelings. This allows you to understand your and others' needs better and respond more effectively.

The last element of the NVC model is clear and concrete requests for action. Developing specific and actionable steps is the core outcome of successfully using NVC.

As you can see, the NVC framework has many benefits. Foundationally, it's an effective communication method that promotes a culture of cooperation and allows for better self-awareness and clarity when expressing thoughts and emotions.

Summary

My clients often ask, " Which model is best for me and the situation I'm dealing with?" There is no simple answer, but it all starts with learning. One reason I recommend these three tools is the vast quantity of information available online. **Start with research; it will go quickly.**

There are also solid books for each, written by the creators of each. Take the time to research and watch online videos (again, there are many to choose from). **Your research aim is to see which resonates with you.** Keep this coaching question in mind: **Which approach matches both your style and approach and the situation?**

More than a few clients found that they **used techniques from each model**. Radical Candor's focus on honest communication and relationship building is a long-term framework, whereas Crucial Conversation is more transactional. Nonviolent communication shares similar traits but is often used as a communication and listening tool.

They all share common traits and are a significant build on dealing with conflict.

- Be aware of your feelings and responses.

- Actively listen to the other person, focusing on what they say versus how you feel when they speak.

- Find common ground and build from it
- Develop action plans based on common ground.
- Agree to continue the dialog.

Learning to deal with conflict rather than avoid it is an essential development area that pays great dividends in the short and long term.

Ambiguity

Challenge 4

Scenario

You join a team in the early stages of a project, and they are stuck. The project mandate is unclear, murky and doesn't seem to be tied to the core mission of the organization.

When questioned, leadership continues to be vague, yet enthusiastic. They want to see what the team can do with a raw idea.

The team struggles to even begin, and the clock is ticking. You feel frustrated and helpless and must figure out a direction or even what initial steps you and the team can take.

Ambiguity can feel like taking steps in a foggy room, even if you aren't sure about directions. The problem with ambiguity is that it impedes job and career success, but you can't avoid it. Like the other challenges in this book, you must understand how to work with it. Because the frequent responses to ambiguity, such as paralysis or indecision, are responses you can control. This chapter aims to give you models and learn to act in the face of ambiguity.

To help understand ambiguity, I want to introduce the VUCA model, which stands for **volatility, uncertainty, complexity, and ambiguity**. Initially created in the military, it's used across business, academia, medicine, and other disciplines. The VUCA framework helps people and organizations understand any challenges posed by an increasingly complex world. Ambiguity is at the core of VUCA.

VUCA DIAGRAM

	Complexity	Volatility
Positive Outcome	Ambiguity	Uncertainty

Current Knowledge

The VUCA framework has four parts with two axes. The horizontal axis defines the current knowledge, and the vertical axis represents the positive outcome. The fourth part is **volatile, which refers to the unpredictable and rapid changes in an external environment**. Because these challenges can be disruptive and sudden, it is more challenging for individuals and companies to respond effectively to them. Volatility is on the upper right of this diagram, which shows that it's the most disruptive.

Then, there's uncertainty below volatility on the lower right side of the diagram. It **involves a need for clarity and predictability about certain**

future events. This means that individuals or companies need access to all the information they need to make informed decisions.

On the upper left side of the diagram, **complexity is described as the interconnected nature of today's problems.** Complex issues might involve problems with many variables, making them complicated to solve.

Last, **ambiguity**, on the lower left side of the diagram, is **information that is unclear or might be open to more than one interpretation**. This often leads to confusion and makes decision-making more complicated.

The primary goal of the VUCA model is to highlight the consequences for people and organizations. For example:

- The ability to adapt to change, which is vital;
- The complexity and uncertainty introduced by risks, but people need to know how to mitigate and manage those risks;
- The need for innovation and creative solutions in the face of complex and ambiguous situations
- Effective leadership in environments where there's a need to guide teams;
- The prioritization of continuous learning and the development of skills
- The building of strong partnerships and a solid network to enhance collaboration and
- Anticipate potential disruptions and build resilience to withstand them.

The VUCA model can have many applications, and some can be used for the challenges highlighted above. For example, you can use this model for strategic planning in the same way that you can use it to assess the external environment and develop strategies that account for ambiguity, complexity, or volatility.

It can also be used for leadership and management. If you are a team leader, this model can inform you about development programs and aid you in navigating some of the highlighted challenges—or even as a crisis management tool that can guide you through crisis response and preparedness efforts.

VUCA is a helpful framework that influences the models and action steps you can take to reduce ambiguity's effect on your work.

Moving From Ambiguity

In the VUCA diagram, ambiguity sits in the lower left corner, typically the worst in a matrix diagram. Ambiguity is almost always a constant and something that clients often deal with. But people can still thrive despite the challenges it brings. Let's talk about three methods you can use to do just that.

Confronting Inertia and Taking Action

One core problem with ambiguity is that it often triggers inertia. This is when you feel stuck and unable to progress because you don't have clear directions or goals. It is crucial that you overcome this locked-up or frozen state so you can move forward.

We are used to having precise paths or specific guiding instructions, so dealing with ambiguity can be overwhelming. Consider the idea of having a compass to help you move past ambiguity. In our digital world, you need to build your GPS, but unlike a GPS that tells us exactly where to go, a compass provides basic orientations such as north, south, east, or west. But with only this, you can start moving away from that ambiguity. Here are some initial steps you can take.

When dealing with ambiguity, you can start by **documenting your basic understanding**—recording what you currently understand about a situation. Documenting this helps you and can be shared with key stakeholders to get their insights and feedback.

You can then **define a small set of actions**. These are used to move out of an ambiguous space. Break down the ambiguity into manageable parts and find a small set of actions where you can start to move away from it.

Often, these **small actions become the building blocks for a more extensive plan**. Also, **brainstorming with your team or end users**, where you collaborate with them to find solutions, is a great way to move away from that ambiguity. Their perspectives can bring in more ideas to help you see the direction you should move in.

These are essential steps to move away from ambiguity. When facing challenges regarding ambiguity and using these initial compass steps, **you see what direction you should move in** and understand that everything is achievable.

There will be times when you will find yourself in a challenging position where you won't be able to use your standard tools, but **learning to leverage what tools and information you have** is essential. Regardless of how small these steps or this progress might be, it's all about taking the first steps to escape this ambiguity. **Taking action is the winning approach.**

Agile, Scrum, and Sprints

Agile scrum is a project management model that allows a team to work in focused, iterative cycles on defined components of a project instead of tackling the entire thing at once. In the scrum vernacular, these cycles **are "sprints," which have a predetermined period and focus on delivering tangible results**. Once a "sprint" finishes, it's evaluated, and whatever insights it provides inform the focus of the next sprint, which might address a different part of the project.

So, what are the benefits of using sprints to minimize ambiguity? Sprints focus on continuous progress, enabling you or the team to see initial results on a project that might be overwhelming. **Sprints promote not needing the whole picture, but you learn as you go.**

This model has an iterative learning component. **With each sprint, you gain valuable insights, which allow you to understand the project better.** You can then refine the project's goal and any challenges and take action on potential solutions.

Sprints also allow you to build on success, regardless of how small that might be. Each completed sprint represents success. The knowledge gained from a prior sprint can guide the following sprints, leading to a more comprehensive and productive outcome.

I want to compare the agile/sprint method to the more traditional waterfall method. I have already discussed the latter, but I'm just going to refresh your memory.

The **waterfall model is a framework that requires each project phase to be completed before proceeding to the next**. It's a rigid structure, especially in an ambiguous situation. The waterfall model often leads to long delays because every element must be completed before proceeding to the next phase.

The agile/sprint method is much more flexible and adaptable because breaking the project into smaller pieces makes it more manageable. Ambiguity becomes an accepted part of complex projects, allowing you to move forward even when unsure.

To sum up, the agile/sprint method is an excellent tool for addressing ambiguity, allowing you or a team to make continuous progress even if they don't have the complete picture. This contrasts with the more rigid and linear way the waterfall method is.

The waterfall model has its place but can stifle progress in an ambiguous project.

Iterative Communication

Iterative communication is also a great way to fence off ambiguity and ensure smooth progress throughout a complex and sometimes overwhelming project. Like many parts of this book, communication is foundational. It's about **having a consistent flow of information and developing shared knowledge**. This allows you or a team to overcome ambiguity. Let's go through the parts.

Ambiguity can exist when certain information is missing or incomplete. However, **iterative communication includes a consistent exchange of information among all involved in the project**. This allows for bridging gaps in the project's understanding or particular tasks, addressing emerging questions, and providing updates. Remember the Johari Window concept I mentioned in the first part of the book? This model is used to understand and improve communication and can play a crucial role in iterative communication.

Johari Window is divided into four areas: **open, hidden, unknown, and blind spot**.

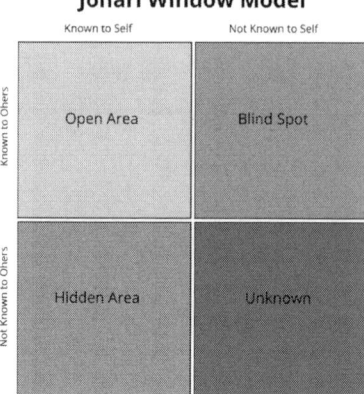

Another way to manage ambiguity is to use the Johari Window and categorize knowledge in terms of time: **past, present, and future**.

Past communication, which documents completed tasks, provides historical context and aids the team in understanding how the project reached its present state.

Present communication is about sharing information about things you and the team are working on informing everyone about ongoing tasks. There's also a need to communicate the present challenges, such as addressing issues, roadblocks, or anything else that might fall into this category. This is important because acknowledging these challenges openly will help you and the rest of the team collaborate and have a higher chance of overcoming them quickly.

Finally, **future communication** outlines the following steps, actions, and ultimate project goals. This sets expectations for what is yet to come and clarifies the team's trajectory and project. As the project progresses, the clarity of the goals improves, and these also need to be communicated.

The primary goal of iterative communication is to mitigate and reduce ambiguity by allowing shared knowledge among project participants.

Looking at communication through the Johari Window and recognizing the goal is to expand the open area, the top right quadrant. The more information is in the open area, the more you and the team comprehensively understand the project's goal and complexity. This larger open area ultimately allows you and your team to make more informed decisions.

Summary

Throughout this chapter, the emphasis is on taking action. Using the sprint method from the Agile method gives you an approach to acting. Even if the initial step is research, you have a starting point.

Agile also gives you defined, planned cycles or sprints to complete tasks. The goal is to build on each successful sprint and keep moving.

Like all challenges, communication is a core action step. Iterative communication is key. The Johari Window model reduces both the hidden and unknown knowledge elements of a project.

Also, applying a past, present, and future model to your reporting gives you a simple model to share status and direction. This should also encourage more comprehensive understanding, buy-in, and dialogue among the project stakeholders.

Teaming these models together is a proven approach to move from ambiguity to delivery.

Prioritization and Negotiation

Challenge 5

Scenario

Your first few months have gone by quickly and you developing a reputation as a solid contributor and team member. Leadership has provided positive feedback (which feels good) but they also are handing you more tasks and responsibilities (which give you mixed feelings).

In a recent interaction with your boss, you're presented with a new project that is a high priority. You have learned enough to know this is time-consuming and you're not sure how you will fit it into your already full plate.

You want to be successful, but the workload is now daunting, and you are not sure how to communicate your concerns or even develop an action plan.

This scenario is common in organizations today, especially when more work is expected from fewer people. Typical team responses range from emotional outbursts to quiet and reluctant acceptance.

Learning to respond effectively to changing situations requires a clear picture of your current workload and then offering thoughtful, realistic options to your leaders. I'll share tools and models so you can quickly learn and apply them. Then, we'll use practical negotiation approaches from the Harvard Program on Negotiations.

Prioritization and Negotiation are the foundations of self-advocacy in a new job. Learning to speak for yourself effectively is a must for your career.

Let's begin with the initial step: assessing your current workload.

Assessing Your Current Workload

When asked to take on more, it's essential to understand your workload. To do that, more than identifying all the tasks and projects you and your team are currently engaged in is required. You also have to understand the underlying factors that are driving this workload. This is where capacity planning comes in because it gives you a much more comprehensive perspective on the work you are facing.

Capacity Planning

You can use this tool to evaluate your and your team's current state and estimate future work demands. Here, you can divide this approach into five distinct steps. They are:

- **Forecast expected demand**: predict the demand for projects that might come your way. This is anything from customer requests to upcoming initiatives.

- **Determine required capacity**: calculate the resources and effort needed to complete the projects you are already working on and the potential future work. To do this, you need a thorough analysis of the requirements of future projects and the entire team's capabilities when working on them.

- **Understand the current capacity**: here, you get a better idea of your team's limits by looking at the time, skills, and resources.

- **Measure the capacity gap:** this is the required extra workload that you and the team cannot adjust to without making changes.

- **Align the capacity with expected demand**: The plan may comprise several elements, such as prioritization, allocation of resources, or even process improvements.

As you read this, it may be a brief introduction to an MBA class. This process may be challenging, especially when new to a role or organization. But it's worth the effort.

I'm sharing it to give you an idea of the components you will need to develop when negotiating the workload for you and your team. Expect this to be a manageable skill, but consider the elements as you confront these issues.

Impact of Added Work

It is also essential to recognize the impact of the added work on you and the team. This can have consequences not only for the team's productivity but also for their morale. Overloading yourself or your team with more work often leads to burnout, which can additionally decrease the quality of work output and job satisfaction. If you are talking to leadership about the potential consequences, highlight the importance of capacity planning and alignment.

When tasked with another project and you and the rest of the team are already at capacity, look at things strategically and use data to help you thoroughly analyze the capacity planning. With this, you can find out the workload, identify gaps, build a significant case for alignment, and communicate any potential consequences of overloading the team.

Initially, this may feel like extra work with little reward. I encourage you to try this in chunks. 10% of your schedule is a good time investment that can generate significant payback.

Building Alignment

Once you have figured out the capacity needed, you must align with the increased workload, which requires collaboration. While a conversation might suffice, and you can get everyone on board, your chances improve if you present a well-documented case outlining the capacity planning findings, such as the capacity gap and your alignment proposal. You or the rest of the team might be happier about some changes, so you must be prepared for that conversation and know the benefits those changes might bring.

Plan and Communicate

An effective workload is crucial for managing or working on an overloaded team. It would help if you had gathered and analyzed capacity data, so the next step should be to make a prioritization plan.

This plan should help with interactions between management and team members and aid you in making compelling requests for any adjustments that need to be made. Here are some approaches you can take.

First, **your action plan should prioritize the necessary adjustments to align capacity with demand**. There are a few things that you can do. If one of the current project deadlines conflicts with the new workload, you can propose a change of delivery dates. This ensures the proposed timeline is realistic and aligns with the team's capabilities. You can also shift resources by evaluating this allocation across the different projects. For instance, you can do it if some projects can have resources temporarily reallocated to a new project, compromising no deadlines or other commitments. You can also add additional resources if the workload exceeds the team's current capacity. This could be adding new team members or contractors or outsourcing.

Then, you should **present your requests effectively so they are as persuasive as possible**. To do this, you must back them up with data and the benefits of implementing the proposed changes. You can explain what the team can achieve if the proposal is accepted. Emphasize the positive outcomes and how those changes might align with the organization's goals more broadly.

> I've learned that attending meetings is an art and a science. I now dedicate a lot more time than I thought I would to okay this meeting's coming up. Who exactly should be in it and why? Because you always have to have a balance.
>
> JAMES TANG, CEO | FORMER CFO

Even if you are confident about your proposal, it is always good practice to have a Plan B. You can share it later, especially if you expect resistance to your first request. However, having a Plan B also shows leadership that you are flexible but committed to finding a solution that works. Planning and communicating are essential to managing or working on an overloaded team. Transforming capacity data into a well-structured action plan will allow you to make your requests more interesting. By presenting it, having a contingency plan, and highlighting the benefits, you can increase the likelihood of successfully aligning capacity with demand and ensuring the team's success.

The Four Negotiating Approaches

Regardless of what it is, negotiating in your role can feel uncomfortable. But to grow in your career, this is a skill that you must have. Over two decades of negotiations as a recruiting leader and executive coach taught me this area produces incredible rewards for those who learn it well. Yet many of my clients find it intimidating, and I have seen many avoid negotiating and settling for an initial offer. While I'll expand on the four negotiating approaches, **there are five because avoiding Negotiation is, unfortunately, a negotiation tactic.**

Collaborative Approach

The collaborative approach, also known as **"win-win" Negotiation, is when the two sides actively work together to find a solution that benefits everyone involved**. This approach involves open communication, problem-solving, and a focus on the shared interests of both parties. When pursuing this approach, you and whoever you are negotiating with assume that there are solutions that can satisfy everyone. This is a critical negotiation approach if you're trying to preserve the relationship; this is almost always true, given the context. Remember that long-term mutual gains are usually more valuable than short-term wins for either party. It is also important to highlight that this approach is efficient when both sides have common goals, which is also almost always the case in the context I'm talking about.

I used this method for over two decades as a recruiting leader in thousands of job offer negotiations. I also share the collaborative model with my clients as their coach as a proven way to get the best possible offer and build an effective relationship.

Competing Approach

A competitive negotiation is also known as a **"win-lose"** and is one of the most common forms of Negotiation. Here, **one or both parties strive to maximize their gains without considering the other side**. If you go for this type of Negotiation, you need to be assertive, think strategically, and even use power plays. Here, people also assume that there are limited resources, so the gains of one party come at the expense of the losses of the other. In a work environment, this differs from my negotiation approach; however, you might have to use it at some point. For instance, it is vital when you need to protect your interests or achieve your immediate goals.

Compromising Approach

The compromising negotiation approach is similar to the collaborative negotiation approach, with a significant difference: **By trying to reach a middle ground, both parties make concessions to find a suitable solution for both sides, while in a collaborative approach, rarely are any concessions made, or if they are, there are other things to gain.**

Compromising usually involves the willingness to give up on some of your goals as long as the other party does, **but it assumes neither side can fully achieve what they want.** I would only use this strategy when there are time constraints, like insufficient time to find a win-win situation for both sides or other external pressures that demand a quick resolution. You still want to maintain a good relationship with the other side. It's a solid approach when a win-win outcome isn't possible.

Accommodating Approach

This tactic, also known as **"lose-win" negotiation**, happens **when you prioritize the other party's interests more than your own.** To pursue this negotiation type, you must have empathy, be selfless, and believe that keeping the relationship is more important than your needs. While it is not an ideal practice, if you think preserving the relationship is more important than the immediate outcome and there's no win-win outcome, consider it. It is also good if your gain is unimportant and you want to build trust with the other side.

Obviously, the collaborative negotiation approach, or win-win, is the tactic I encourage you to strive for as often as possible. However, situations sometimes don't allow that to happen, in which case you might have to go for one of the other tactics.

If you want to become a skilled negotiator, you should be able to understand and apply any of these strategies. Remember, having a successful negotiation is about your gains and building or maintaining a relationship.

Summary

This may feel overwhelming in the first year of a new job, and it is. These frameworks should be integrated into your career tool chest.

Developing a solid sense of your workload and capacity is necessary, especially as your tasks and responsibilities grow. Saying no or challenging back without a model to do that can set you back. Learning about Capacity Planning and applying it to your work is essential.

It is about having a powerful picture of what you can effectively deliver and offering fact-based options when the workload becomes unwieldy. This is where the development of presentation and persuasion skills are essential. Work on this as you grow in your job.

Understanding negotiations is a must-learn skill. You probably already figured out that Negotiation is a core tool. Develop these skills by first using them in low-risk situations. Enhance them and ramp up your use of them.

Prioritization and Negotiation are the last of the five challenges because they involve the most work – and usually come later in your new job success. It also builds your ability to self-advocate. Finally, this challenge bridges the next phase of your new job success: Building Expertise.

DEVELOPING EXPERTISE

✓ PRESENCE AND BRAND

✓ THE BALANCING ACT

✓ JOURNAL

Presence and Brand

Scenario

As you progress in your new job, you may notice small feedback points you're receiving. More than once, team members have called you the "go-to person" for a specific task or knowledge area. They have also described you as "quiet but efficient".

These are nice comments, but they don't reflect your desire to master a complex process within the organization. You want to be viewed as someone who can provide a deeper contribution, thought leadership on a topic or potentially leading teams. You want to grow, be respected, and have an upward trajectory in your career.

The challenge you face is how to develop and manage an authentic public persona that reflects that. Making those adjustments might feel awkward; you don't want to show off. But having people see these competencies is important to your career goals.

As you move through the first 6 to 9 months of your new job, you are probably doing well with your Game Planning and learning to manage the Five Challenges. You are growing in the role and gaining valuable experiences and skills. But developing and nurturing your presence is an afterthought. How you show up in a job is the growth area. But devoting time to your presence and brand is an important step, especially after accomplishing so much using the first two approaches.

Your persona comes from the many things you do, such as your interactions with your colleagues, how you present yourself, or how you engage with organizational cultures. Your public persona in the office often determines how the people around you see you, such as whether you are a great collaborator, a team player, and a potential good leader. Often this persona will affect on your professional growth.

Your persona is based on who you are at your core. It is not a mask or an act; It should be consistent traits you present in your role. Your persona should not be a fake model you can only maintain for short bursts. Everyone has bad days, and those are expected. Your public persona is who you are regularly. It's also something you monitor and seek to improve.

All of this leads to the reputation you have in the workplace, and an authentic, self-aware persona can improve your reputation and open the doors for many other opportunities.

When these all align, you build trust among your colleagues and leadership, which translates into a positive persona. Bottom line: your actions are the core to your persona.

Goal Setting to Enhance your Persona

When defining your public persona, you can take some earlier work we've done and develop it further. Using the baseline KPI's from your Game Plan we can use those to both self-reflect and set enhanced career goals. With this new job experience, you are likely to better understand yourself, your values, and your professional goals. Your upfront work makes it easier for you to adjust your behaviors and actions and align them with your authentic persona.

Start with using self-reflection to look at your strengths and weaknesses. Here, you are looking at your beliefs and how you can translate them into your public persona. You might also pull in your experiences and assess what you learned from them. This self-reflection may happen over several months, starting several months or after you've started the new role or job.

Next, look at your career goals, not only the short-term ones, but also your goals that are more distant or aspirational. This is important because you should tailor your public persona according to these. I refer to these to as your "future state"; you can incorporate elements of them into your persona now, even if the goals are in progress.

For instance, if you want to become a team leader or manager, but aren't there yet, you can bring leadership attributes into your persona now. For example, you could focus on being more of an active listener or seek more consensus from your peers and teams. Bring your "future state" into your "present state".

Your personal values should be consistent with your public persona. Understand your core values and beliefs, since these will better define the persona you want to bring forward. A key coaching question to ask is: **"What do you value in your career?"**

Melding your values with your goals is an important next step. With them melded, you can start defining actions and behaviors to give credibility to your persona.

Taking the earlier goal of becoming a leader, you can create actionable steps and strategies to execute. These could improve your communication skills, delegation skills, or deeper expertise in tools and processes. Look for these opportunities to expand your contribution .

Again, these actions and strategies should be flexible in the changing environment of your workplace. Seeking feedback can be a good idea, from colleagues, leaders and coaches needs to be a consistent action step. Feedback is an important loop in your persona, because it can give you observational data on their perception or your actions and presence.

Self-reflection is important to regularly to evaluate your own progress. Keeping a journal, which I've included at the end of the book, can be a powerful tool. Tracking your self-assessments and keeping note of your development will help you identify areas to improve both your actions and your persona. Don't forget that your public persona is an authentic presentation of you and your core values. Staying true to yourself and presenting that is a key step in your job and career.

Understanding the Workplace Culture

Having a good understanding of the workplace culture will help you manage and enhance your public persona. As you know, a workplace culture involves many elements, such as behaviors, shared values, and norms. So, understanding these will give you a much better idea of how you can behave and perform actions. Let's see how you can make a good assessment of the workplace culture as a new employee.

First, you consider doing a cultural assessment. This is fairly simple, but might take some time. For example, pay attention to how your colleagues interact with one another, collaborate, and communicate. You should also look at the company's core values or mission statement to better understand the "written" rules of the culture. With this, you will have a better idea of what is acceptable and what isn't. Then, you look at your own core values and see how they align with the company's and its culture.

But you might adapt and integrate some values. Perhaps you will also have to align your communication style or decision-making process with the cultural expectations of the workplace so you can establish trust with your colleagues. I'm not suggesting you take on values that conflict with your own. You are looking for ways to better align your personal values with the organizations that feel authentic.

Pay attention to cultural nuances or other more pronounced differences within the organization. Try to understand that there are different cultures and workplaces are diverse. Showing respect for all cultural perspectives can allow you to build trust, too. Don't be afraid to ask for help or guidance from colleagues if you're struggling to understand the workplace culture; it might be more obscure than you thought. Don't let the frustration stop you from continuing to understand.

Another thing to keep in mind regarding culture in the workplace is it's shaped by internal or external factors. Pay attention to any shifts that occur in the organization's culture and be able to adapt your persona to them. You can also contribute to the company's culture by enhancing its cultural dynamics. This can be anything from organizing to taking part in activities, projects, or initiatives that promote the workplace's culture.

Growing Your Public Persona

Now, let's explore different ways you can build your public persona. I have already mentioned self-reflection, which is the start of everything, along with goal setting for the persona you want others to perceive. With this, you also built your brand, essentially, a small representation of your expertise and skills and anything else that might set you apart in your line of work. Your brand is a synopsis of your public persona. Being able to articulate your brand is important to your career success. Fortunately, we have covered nearly all the steps earlier in this book.

Try this: think about how you want others to perceive you in your new workplace. To properly grow a public persona and build your brand, consistency is key. Your behaviors, actions, and the way you communicate are in line with the image you want others to perceive.

In the meantime, continue building relationships because the more you build these relationships, the more you can showcase your skills. Communication is a big part of how people perceive you, so it is important that you work on your verbal and written communication skills.

Taking initiative is yet another way to showcase your persona (or you) to others so they can start building an impression of you. Here, you can either propose solutions, volunteer for projects, or look for opportunities where you can showcase everything you want people to see.

But none of this is worth it if the results are not there. Your brand or public persona is also built on your ability to deliver results. Here, you have to be consistent in the delivery of results because these are achievements whose impact you can share, which improves your reputation.

Summary

It is not only important to build your persona but also to manage it. This is an ongoing process requiring flexibility. Again, consistency is vital and your persona should be consistent in across your actions and communication. Having high emotional intelligence is relevant in managing your persona because if you understand your and others' emotions, you can better navigate the intricate dynamics between people and respond appropriately to every circumstance.

Continually reinforcing your brand by delivering results is a proven way to enhance your persona. Managing your reputation by actively managing not only your persona in the workplace but also online applies to the outside world.

When conflicts arise, develop the skills to address them professionally while showing empathy. Conflicts are natural occurrences in the workplace, but how you manage them will show others the person you are.

Last, you also have to show growth as your career moves on. This means that your persona isn't static and reflects the growth you have made throughout your career.

The Balancing Act

Expertise 2

Scenario

You're in the latter part of your first year in your new job. It's gone well, with consistent recognition, good relationships throughout the organization and a sense of pride in your contributions. The problem lies in the workload. Maintaining the quality of your work required increasing your hours work, just to keep up.

At first, the longer hours was a short term solution, but several months passed and your work hours actually increased. You get up early to answer emails, write reports or even jump on calls after dinner. Weekends, especially Sunday are "planning and prep" days.

Personal relationships are taking a hit, you aren't exercising as much and you feel more tired than usual. You love all the rewards in your work, but the treadmill isn't slowing down.

I briefly mentioned the balancing act in other chapters of this book. However, a dedicated chapter should give more weight to this essential and holistic approach to helping you succeed professionally and personally.

There's been a mindset change lately regarding balancing our work and personal lives, as there should be, but balancing is a perpetual project. As I have mentioned, the balancing act comprises four aspects: **professional life, personal life, physical well-being,** and **mental well-being**. Understanding and managing these four components consistently is the cornerstone of a fulfilled life. Here are three concepts based on approaches I witnessed clients adopt and excel at to assist you on this journey. These concepts include **acknowledging Workaholism, cultivating sacred tasks and times**, and **creating accountability**.

Balance = Addressing Workaholism

Achieving equilibrium requires a hard look at Workaholism, which I'm regrettably quite familiar with. It was evident during my college years and followed me throughout my career. In the last decade, I have made significant progress in addressing, finally achieving a sense of balance that gives me a lot of joy and satisfaction.

However, I cannot say the same for some clients I have worked with. Many of these knowledgeable people with remarkable drive overdid and pushed them to exhaustion because of Workaholism. It's a continual theme my clients address in our work.

I remember a particular moment when I saw my Workaholism through the lens of a coach. I was juggling multiple commitments: working 60 hours a week, competing in racquetball, enrolling in a graduate coaching program, and co-leading programs and coaching at Wharton Business School, all at the same time.

Then came a moment that served as a wake-up call. On a weekday, I was on a BART train at 9:30 at night and reading a book called Chained to the Desk, a study of Workaholism.

I had been at work for countless hours, and it suddenly struck me how absurd this lifestyle had become. That moment prompted me to take purposeful steps toward self-improvement.

Workaholism and achieving a balanced life are at opposite ends of the spectrum. If Workaholism dominates your life, you cannot have a balanced life. I speak from firsthand experience when I say that evaluating the four vital elements of your life—professional, personal, physical, and mental well-being—and finding a good balance is foundational.

The first step is to acknowledge that you might struggle with Workaholism. My turning point was on that BART train, but it has yet to be straightforward, like any other significant change in our lives. I have encountered setbacks, failures, and successes along the way. However, time, effort, and consistency helped me progress.

I have seen many of my clients regain their equilibrium, too. For some, seeking therapy in addition to coaching has been met with success toward recovery and balance.

Sacred Tasks and Sacred Times

Another lynchpin to a balanced life is sacred tasks and sacred times. These revolve around cultivating healthy habits, which lead to finding equilibrium.

One of my sacred times is walking at Lake Chabot in the San Francisco Bay Area. This is a way to create a sacred space in my schedule. As I grew older and struggled with Workaholism, I slowly transitioned into a healthier routine. Two years ago, I decided not to work or do coaching sessions on Wednesdays. I also find time to do other activities such as exercising, reading, writing, and, most importantly, relaxing. However, this change in my schedule took some time, but Wednesdays are my sacred day.

I understand that for some of us, blocking an entire day from our calendar is an impossible thing to do. I know I couldn't have done it ten years ago. But I also understood that I could create pockets of time during my week, contributing similarly to a more balanced life. For instance, I was part of a racquetball league, which served as a tremendous sacred time.

The fact that I knew I had only two nights a week for racquetball was gratifying. It combined social interaction, physical activity, and mental well-being, which served me well while working full-time.

Another sacred task I do on Wednesdays is swimming. Swimming is not only a great workout but also a meditative experience. I often share this experience with my wife, which makes it a delightful activity.

Do you have any sacred tasks or sacred times in your life? It's okay if you don't. However, this might be an excellent time to think about creating one or both. Identify any sacred tasks or activities you enjoy and make time for them. Remember, the goal is to lead a balanced life, and establishing and honoring sacred tasks and sacred times is a significant starting point.

Accountability Partners

The trickiest part of the balancing act is dealing with the inevitable regression and sliding backward that we all go through when trying to make a significant shift in our lives. One of the most critical components of achieving a successful balance is accountability. Ten years ago, I was lucky enough to have an accountability partner in one of my colleagues, Shirley. We shared a workspace, and Shirley possessed an impressive ability to accomplish tasks efficiently. She also served as a central figure whom everyone in HR respected and turned to with their inquiries. The dynamic of our team was excellent, but Shirley contributed something extra: accountability. Although we worked seamlessly as a team, she had noted my consistently late hours at work.

Instead of intrusively prying into my affairs, she would quietly ask several times a week, "What time are you leaving tonight?" This seemingly straightforward question prompted me to reflect on the time dedicated to my job. Although I still face challenges, having Shirley and my wife monitor my work schedule proved immensely helpful.

Accountability with a friend, coach, or any other professional can be a powerful tool to balance your life. So, here's a coaching question for you: What would you like to improve in your balancing act? And how would accountability help?

The Balancing Act in Three Parts

While I'm going to discuss three concepts, I'm going to shift the discussion to the physical, mental, social/emotional, and spiritual, which will help you balance the four components of the balancing act. While the physical and mental directly relate to the physical and mental well-being of the balancing act, the social/emotional and spiritual link to all four components of the act.

An optimal, balanced life means being healthy in all aspects. Enter the three concepts/focus areas.

Physical Balance

Physical well-being usually involves three components: **exercise, nutrition, and stress management.** If you need to get into exercising, you can start walking during your sacred times. Starting slow is not an issue; you can start with short walks, increase from there, and if you feel like it, start running, go to the gym, or do any physical activity you enjoy.

Nutrition is also important, and I know many of us face weight management challenges. It's also a personal challenge. There are several approaches to this, and the best place to start is tracking.

Using apps like MyFitnessPal, Lose It!, or Lifesum are good starting points. They track your food intake and calories and add exercise and activity tracking.

Another crucial aspect of physical well-being is **sleep**. Having a proper night of sleep is the cornerstone of maintaining health. Here, planning your sleeping schedule is just as important. There will be nights when your sleep won't be as good, especially if you don't have a good sleeping pattern, and that's fine. However, focus on optimizing your sleep when you have the time to do it.

The best way to plan your sleep is to start by structuring your time around sleeping. This means finding out what time you want to wake up and working back to ensure you have the recommended eight hours of sleep.

Six different areas can help you plan your sleep more effectively (Mayo Clinic Staff, 2020):

1. Please set up a consistent sleep schedule and stick to it.
2. Be mindful of what you drink and eat, especially before bedtime.
3. Create a sleep-conducive environment.
4. Limit any daytime naps to prevent disrupting your sleep at night.
5. Incorporate physical activity into your daily routine.
6. Incorporate stress management techniques to decrease anxiety and stress.

Tracking your sleep with a smartwatch or even smart rings like Oura can raise your sleep awareness and prompt you to take action as outlined above.

Managing your stress is yet another important component of your physical well-being. You can use many resources to make it easier to integrate stress-reduction activities into your life. Meditation is a great way to do it; in this case, even essential mindfulness is a great tool. It is easy; let me give you an example.

First, you must find a comfortable sitting position and ensure your back is straight. Then, it would help if you focused on your breathing, whether in the contraction of your belly or chest or the simple sensation of breathing through your nose. Your mind will inevitably wander, so you must gently bring it back to focus on breathing. As with everything else, you might find it hard to do it initially, but as you continue, you will improve and increase the time you spend practicing mindfulness. Even a mere five minutes of this can have health benefits. There's no right or wrong way to meditate as long as you are comfortable. Focus on your breathing, and gradually, as you get better, increase the time you meditate.

There are many free meditation apps, but the best I have used are Headspace or Calm. They provide both free and premium versions, and they are excellent for getting started and growing a meditation practice.

Mental Balance

Achieving mental well-being can be divided into four major activities: **having fun, exploring interesting things, and learning**. Consider incorporating these components into your daily life, much like meditation.

Note that each of these three areas is equally important. Approach them in a balanced way. Let's have a look at them, starting with fun.

The fun part is all about indulging in content you find entertaining; whether it is books, TV shows, movies, or music, it is entirely up to you. You can use this time to catch up on some of your guilty pleasures and set aside some binge-watching time. The focus on fun will be looked at again shortly in the social balance section. But again, maintain a balance between your own choices.

Then, there's the **exciting category**, which involves exploring things related to other interests. This could also be entertainment, such as documentaries, trying out a new dish or cuisine, or even reading books from a genre you haven't read before. While this should be enjoyable, it should also be exploratory.

The last component is **learning**. Here, your focus should be on acquiring knowledge or skills, such as learning a new language, mastering cooking different dishes, or learning a new skill, perhaps in a new language in music or even art. Remember that this is your sacred time, so don't overdo it.

Let me give you some ideas if you need help figuring out where to start. Investigate the NY Times Bestseller List, Amazon Bestsellers, or USA Today's Bestseller List for book recommendations. If you have specific interests, such as fantasy, sci-fi, or romance, you can delve into websites such as Amazon that categorize these genres in myriad ways.

For visual content, such as TV shows, movies, or documentaries, any streaming giants, such as Netflix and Amazon Prime, have a lot of content you can look for in different genres.

Online learning might be a great option. Platforms such as Udemy or Coursera have a wide range of options. LinkedIn Learning also has a wide range, but its content is anchored in Skills development. The important thing here is to focus on well-being strategies and look for content that you will enjoy, and that will offer you a more balanced life.

Social and Emotional Well-Being

Being socially and emotionally "healthy" is a big part of the balancing act. It features four areas: **service, empathy, synergy, and intrinsic security**. This model is part of Stephen Covey's 7 Habits of Highly Successful People. We will look at each to understand how it can better balance your life.

Service is quite a basic concept but has tremendous implications. It is all about acting for the benefit of others. Here, what should drive you is the willingness to contribute to something or help someone expecting no reward. In business, this is often called servant leadership, and it focuses on giving instead of solely thinking about personal gain. Service aligns with current leadership trends, where leaders prioritize service to their teams and organizations to help them succeed.

We can divide service into three categories: **immediate, short-term, and long-term.** The first category concerns actions that have an immediate positive impact. For example, tell one of your colleagues you're going to print something for yourself, and that you can bring the copies they printed when you're back, so they don't have to waste time walking to the copy machine. Small actions where you have nothing to gain often yield immediate positive impacts.

That's short-term service, where you create small wins for others. This often involves doing something for someone else or helping without being asked.

Last, there's long-term service, which involves more planning and execution. These are often more meaningful and require more time and effort, but the positive impact is also more impactful.

It would help if you tried to incorporate immediate service actions into your life, both inside and outside of work, which will promote your social and emotional well-being. Many of these can be simple gestures, such as holding the door for someone or checking in on a friend or neighbor. This shows genuine kindness and empathy. From there, start incorporating short-term and long-term service actions into your life, and I'm optimistic you'll improve your overall well-being.

> I'm committed to being the best parent as my kids, aged 9 and 6 are growing up fast. I only have five more years before my opportunity to spend time with them starts to diminish. This lines up with when I have the highest earning potential, and even though it's a trade-off, I'm happy to make it. F inding meaning beyond work is critical for mental health.
>
> DANIEL CHEN FINTECH EXEC | START-UP CEO | INVESTOR

Empathy is a vital aspect of social and emotional well-being, and it revolves around the deep understanding of others' experiences, perspectives, and emotions. It is not only understanding; it is exploring the world of genuine human connection. Empathy requires acknowledging their situation and immersing yourself in their perspective. When you can do this, you have a great tool to connect with people on a deeper level, which helps you build connections with them. From here, this connection can only get more profound, which improves communication and many other things.

Having this sense of empathy can also help with conflict resolution because you can empathize with the perspectives and feelings of other people and find common ground faster.

However, one of the best benefits of developing empathy is reducing stress. By empathizing with others, you can improve your capacity for managing stress.

Synergy is another concept that can enhance your social and emotional well-being. Working together harmoniously almost always leads to better outcomes. Synergy contributes to many things that happen in the workplace. For example, people will collaborate more through synergy, combining their skills and strengths to reach the same goal. Creativity improves with synergy because when there's synergy between different people from different backgrounds and perspectives, ideas flow better and are broader.

Working with people in synergy also gives you a better sense of belonging. Collaborating provides this sense of community and social connection, which contributes to your social and emotional well-being. It also improves communication, conflict resolution, and empathy toward others.

There's also **intrinsic security**, which encompasses a person's inner strength and capability to overcome challenges without relying excessively on others or external circumstances or validation. But this intrinsic security is the culmination of the other aspects we've discussed here.

It brings authenticity because you are more likely to embrace yourself; it improves your emotional resilience and self-reliance. With this, you can not only better manage your stress but also improve your self-compassion and foster a positive image of yourself. Intrinsic security is about self-confidence, authenticity, and emotional resilience.

You can better decide to stay true to your principles even when facing challenges.

Summary

When you pursue a balanced and fulfilling life, prioritize and nurture these aspects. Physical well-being gives you strength; mental well-being gives you creativity and intellect; social and emotional well-being allows you to connect with others on a deeper level; and spiritual well-being gives you inner peace.

However, notice that most Balancing Acts are best when done with others. You have your sacred times and sacred tasks, which can be solo activities, but much of your Balancing Act involves developing and growing meaningful relationships.

Nurturing meaningful relationships was hit hard by the pandemic, and we are still recovering from that. Many of my clients at all career levels experience loneliness. The Balancing Act is a vital part of your career and personal success.

Together, this gives you the framework for a fulfilled life, but invest time in each aspect as you strive for overall well-being.

Journaling

Expertise 3

One of my pet peeves about self-help books is that they often give you great ideas and then end there. In the book I co-wrote with Steve Hernandez, The Job Search Manifesto, we added workbook elements that our readers received and appreciated. I will do the same thing here. The following pages are a one-year journal to support you as you integrate the ideas in this book.

Note to Ebook readers: You will find all the journaling page samples on my site: https://www.mikecoach.com/new-job-success-book

Journaling is where you can monitor your journey and make more minor changes that almost always lead to continued progress. You need an idea of the actions you are doing both well and poorly to improve. When my clients transition into a new role, we often focus on the same key areas to ensure their success. The goal of the Journal is quite simple:

- Keep yourself on course.

- Assess your progress as often as you can.

- Make minor and manageable adjustments instead of large and dramatic ones.

The Journal in this book revolves around coaching models and ideas. I broke it down into sections that follow the book's format.

The New Job Success Journal uses a method called Bullet Journaling. Developed by Ryder Carroll, bullet journaling uses brief entries to show status. They called this rapid logging. We can group entries into "collections" to capture related tasks, notes, and ideas. (Bulletjournal.com, 2023)

I've layered in the key ideas from the book, along with solid coaching principles, to make the New Job Success Journal easy to use but insightful as you move through your initial year on the job.

The Journal's Structure

I broke the Journal into these sections:

- Weekly Summary
- Monthly Summary
- Wins / Successes
- Learning
- Value Delivered
- Relationship Building
- Challenges
- Goals
- Balancing Act

Weekly tracking for the first three months of your new job is fundamental because your focus is on quickly learning and adapting to the new position. You can stay agile and make immediate adjustments as you adapt to your new role by tracking your progress weekly.

In the weekly tracking, declare your focus for that week. At the end of the week, there is a one through five assessment of how well you achieved your focus. This is a simple way to keep your "eye on the ball." Expect your ability to accomplish this to fluctuate, especially in the first few weeks.

Monthly tracking takes you through the rest of the year, which is essential because you are settling in after the initial period. Tracking your progress every month can give you a longer perspective. This way, you can assess your progress from a broader perspective and understand and identify trends and patterns in your performance.

Wins or Successes come next. There is separate tracking for challenges, but wins are so important that they have their list. I did this because my clients often lose track of early wins, and it's a scramble in the future to go back and remember and recapture them. Also, seeing a list of your wins is a great way to keep yourself motivated, particularly in your first year.

Learning is a critical part of your career, especially in the first year, and having a log or Journal of what you learned can boost your effectiveness and planning. Over time, this list should guide you in what lessons come next.

Value delivered is core in the game plan section of this book, and journaling what you've delivered also helps frame out your first year. Much like learning, seeing a list of your offers can help you spot growth patterns and future career interests.

Relationship building is the heart of your career, and keeping a log is really important. This is especially true in your first year so you can see which individuals are key influencers in your success. Sometimes, those people who strongly influence you are not your boss. Journaling and tracking this can help spot that.

The **Challenges** section will cover four challenges: failure, conflict, ambiguity, prioritization, and scaling. Like the other journal areas, spotting patterns here is a key takeaway.

Goals help you map your long-term plans to specific actions and outcomes. In this book, goal setting takes place a few months after you begin so you can incorporate your new job experience into your goals.

Effective Journaling

Using the bullet journal model will take time, but consistency is essential. Some clients found using it daily was helpful. My pace was about twice a week, for 10 to 15 minutes each time. I use it towards the end of Fridays to capture a snapshot of my week. Find the best way for you to use the Journal consistently and regularly.

Periodically, reflect on your performance and growth in a more expansive way. As you look back through your Journal, ask yourself questions such as:

- **What are my key areas of progress?**
- **What strengths have I developed, and**
- **Where can I improve next?**

This type of self-assessment keeps you accountable and looking forward to what you should do next to improve.

Revisiting and reviewing your Journal will allow you to determine whether it aligns with your goals and the company's goals and whether you can grow and adapt professionally.

Taking this approach will not only make you help you better at your job but will also promote and develop skills you can improve, which will help you progress in your career. Invest the time to journal; the results will be significant.

JOB SUCCESS JOURNAL WEEKLY SUMMARY

WEEK ____

WEEKLY FOCUS

End of Week Results: **1 2 3 4 5**

TOP 10 ACTIVITIES

CATEGORY	#	DESCRIPTION	FOLLOW UP

Categories

L - Learning	C - Conflict
RB - Relationship Building	A - Ambiguity
DV - Deliver Value	PN - Prioritization & Negotiation
W - Wins/Success	G - Goals
F - Failure	BA - Balancing Act

Time Study

What categories did I spend the most time on?

1	
2	
3	
4	
5	

COACHING QUESTIONS

- What worked well this week?
- What do I want to improve on next week?
- What Categories will I emphasize next week?

JOB SUCCESS JOURNAL WEEKLY SUMMARY

WEEK ____

WEEKLY FOCUS

End of Week Results: **1 2 3 4 5**

TOP 10 ACTIVITIES

CATEGORY	#	DESCRIPTION	FOLLOW UP

Categories

L - Learning	C - Conflict
RB - Relationship Building	A - Ambiguity
DV - Deliver Value	PN - Prioritization & Negotiation
W - Wins/Success	G - Goals
F - Failure	BA - Balancing Act

Time Study

What categories did I spend the most time on?

1	
2	
3	
4	
5	

COACHING QUESTIONS

- What worked well this week?
- What do I want to improve on next week?
- What Categories will I emphasize next week?

JOB SUCCESS JOURNAL WEEKLY SUMMARY

WEEK _____

WEEKLY FOCUS

[   ]

End of Week Results: **1 2 3 4 5**

TOP 10 ACTIVITIES

CATEGORY	#	DESCRIPTION	FOLLOW UP

Categories

L - Learning	C - Conflict
RB - Relationship Building	A - Ambiguity
DV - Deliver Value	PN - Prioritization & Negotiation
W - Wins/Success	G - Goals
F - Failure	BA - Balancing Act

Time Study

What categories did I spend the most time on?

1	
2	
3	
4	
5	

COACHING QUESTIONS

- What worked well this week?
- What do I want to improve on next week?
- What Categories will I emphasize next week?

JOB SUCCESS JOURNAL WEEKLY SUMMARY

WEEK _____

WEEKLY FOCUS

[   ]

End of Week Results: **1 2 3 4 5**

TOP 10 ACTIVITIES

CATEGORY	#	DESCRIPTION	FOLLOW UP

Categories

L - Learning	C - Conflict
RB - Relationship Building	A - Ambiguity
DV - Deliver Value	PN - Prioritization & Negotiation
W - Wins/Success	G - Goals
F - Failure	BA - Balancing Act

Time Study

What categories did I spend the most time on?

1	
2	
3	
4	
5	

COACHING QUESTIONS

- What worked well this week?
- What do I want to improve on next week?
- What Categories will I emphasize next week?

NEW JOB SUCCESS MONTHLY SUMMARY

MONTH ____

Look through the last month and summarize the following areas

WINS

KNOWLEDGE

RELATIONSHIPS

NEW MONTH'S ACTION PLAN

JOB SUCCESS JOURNAL WEEKLY SUMMARY

WEEK ____

WEEKLY FOCUS

End of Week Results: **1 2 3 4 5**

TOP 10 ACTIVITIES

CATEGORY	#	DESCRIPTION	FOLLOW UP

Categories

L - Learning	C - Conflict
RB - Relationship Building	A - Ambiguity
DV - Deliver Value	PN - Prioritization & Negotiation
W - Wins/Success	G - Goals
F - Failure	BA - Balancing Act

Time Study

What categories did I spend the most time on?

1	
2	
3	
4	
5	

COACHING QUESTIONS

- What worked well this week?
- What do I want to improve on next week?
- What Categories will I emphasize next week?

JOB SUCCESS JOURNAL WEEKLY SUMMARY

WEEK ____

WEEKLY FOCUS

[   ]

End of Week Results: **1 2 3 4 5**

TOP 10 ACTIVITIES

CATEGORY	#	DESCRIPTION	FOLLOW UP

Categories

L - Learning	C - Conflict
RB - Relationship Building	A - Ambiguity
DV - Deliver Value	PN - Prioritization & Negotiation
W - Wins/Success	G - Goals
F - Failure	BA - Balancing Act

Time Study

What categories did I spend the most time on?

1	
2	
3	
4	
5	

COACHING QUESTIONS

- What worked well this week?
- What do I want to improve on next week?
- What Categories will I emphasize next week?

JOB SUCCESS JOURNAL WEEKLY SUMMARY

WEEK _____

WEEKLY FOCUS

End of Week Results: **1 2 3 4 5**

TOP 10 ACTIVITIES

CATEGORY	#	DESCRIPTION	FOLLOW UP

Categories

L - Learning	C - Conflict
RB - Relationship Building	A - Ambiguity
DV - Deliver Value	PN - Prioritization & Negotiation
W - Wins/Success	G - Goals
F - Failure	BA - Balancing Act

Time Study

What categories did I spend the most time on?

1	
2	
3	
4	
5	

COACHING QUESTIONS

- What worked well this week?
- What do I want to improve on next week?
- What Categories will I emphasize next week?

JOB SUCCESS JOURNAL WEEKLY SUMMARY

WEEK ____

WEEKLY FOCUS

End of Week Results: **1 2 3 4 5**

TOP 10 ACTIVITIES

CATEGORY	#	DESCRIPTION	FOLLOW UP

Categories

L - Learning	C - Conflict
RB - Relationship Building	A - Ambiguity
DV - Deliver Value	PN - Prioritization & Negotiation
W - Wins/Success	G - Goals
F - Failure	BA - Balancing Act

Time Study

What categories did I spend the most time on?

1	
2	
3	
4	
5	

COACHING QUESTIONS

- What worked well this week?
- What do I want to improve on next week?
- What Categories will I emphasize next week?

NEW JOB SUCCESS MONTHLY SUMMARY

MONTH ____

Look through the last month and summarize the following areas

WINS

KNOWLEDGE

RELATIONSHIPS

NEW MONTH'S ACTION PLAN

JOB SUCCESS JOURNAL WEEKLY SUMMARY

WEEK ____

WEEKLY FOCUS

End of Week Results: **1** 2 3 4 5

TOP 10 ACTIVITIES

CATEGORY	#	DESCRIPTION	FOLLOW UP

Categories

L - Learning	C - Conflict
RB - Relationship Building	A - Ambiguity
DV - Deliver Value	PN - Prioritization & Negotiation
W - Wins/Success	G - Goals
F - Failure	BA - Balancing Act

Time Study

What categories did I spend the most time on?

1	
2	
3	
4	
5	

COACHING QUESTIONS

- What worked well this week?
- What do I want to improve on next week?
- What Categories will I emphasize next week?

JOB SUCCESS JOURNAL WEEKLY SUMMARY

WEEK _____

WEEKLY FOCUS

End of Week Results: **1 2 3 4 5**

TOP 10 ACTIVITIES

CATEGORY	#	DESCRIPTION	FOLLOW UP

Categories

L - Learning	C - Conflict
RB - Relationship Building	A - Ambiguity
DV - Deliver Value	PN - Prioritization & Negotiation
W - Wins/Success	G - Goals
F - Failure	BA - Balancing Act

Time Study

What categories did I spend the most time on?

1	
2	
3	
4	
5	

COACHING QUESTIONS

- What worked well this week?
- What do I want to improve on next week?
- What Categories will I emphasize next week?

JOB SUCCESS JOURNAL WEEKLY SUMMARY

WEEK _____

WEEKLY FOCUS

End of Week Results: **1 2 3 4 5**

TOP 10 ACTIVITIES

CATEGORY	#	DESCRIPTION	FOLLOW UP

Categories

L - Learning	C - Conflict
RB - Relationship Building	A - Ambiguity
DV - Deliver Value	PN - Prioritization & Negotiation
W - Wins/Success	G - Goals
F - Failure	BA - Balancing Act

Time Study

What categories did I spend the most time on?

1	
2	
3	
4	
5	

COACHING QUESTIONS

- What worked well this week?
- What do I want to improve on next week?
- What Categories will I emphasize next week?

JOB SUCCESS JOURNAL WEEKLY SUMMARY

WEEK ____

WEEKLY FOCUS

End of Week Results: **1 2 3 4 5**

TOP 10 ACTIVITIES

CATEGORY	#	DESCRIPTION	FOLLOW UP

Categories

L - Learning	C - Conflict
RB - Relationship Building	A - Ambiguity
DV - Deliver Value	PN - Prioritization & Negotiation
W - Wins/Success	G - Goals
F - Failure	BA - Balancing Act

Time Study

What categories did I spend the most time on?

1	
2	
3	
4	
5	

COACHING QUESTIONS

- What worked well this week?
- What do I want to improve on next week?
- What Categories will I emphasize next week?

NEW JOB SUCCESS MONTHLY SUMMARY

MONTH _____

Look through the last month and summarize the following areas

WINS

KNOWLEDGE

RELATIONSHIPS

NEW MONTH'S ACTION PLAN

WINS

Describe the new learning in a quick summary. Then note the action plan with each win.
Add it to your weekly summary with **W** for the category code..

#	DESCRIPTION	IMPACT
1		
2		
3		
4		
5		
6		
7		
8		
9		
10		
11		
12		

WINS

Describe the new learning in a quick summary. Then note the action plan with each wins.
Add it to your weekly summary with **W** for the category code..

#	DESCRIPTION	IMPACT
13		
14		
15		
16		
17		
18		
19		
20		
21		
22		
23		
24		

NEW JOB SUCCESS LEARNING SUMMARY

Describe the new learning in a quick summary. Then note the action plan with each new learning.
Add it to your weekly summary with L for the category code..

#	DESCRIPTION	ACTION PLAN
1		
2		
3		
4		
5		
6		
7		
8		
9		
10		
11		
12		

NEW JOB SUCCESS LEARNING SUMMARY

Describe the new learning in a quick summary. Then note the action plan with each new learning. Add it to your weekly summary with **L** for the category code..

#	DESCRIPTION	ACTION PLAN
13		
14		
15		
16		
17		
18		
19		
20		
21		
22		
23		
24		

NEW JOB SUCCESS DELIVERED VALUE SUMMARY

Describe the new learning in a quick summary. Then note the action plan with each value delivered.
Add it to your weekly summary with **DV** for the category code.

#	DESCRIPTION	ACTION PLAN
1		
2		
3		
4		
5		
6		
7		
8		
9		
10		
11		
12		
13		
14		
15		
16		
17		
18		
19		
20		

NEW JOB SUCCESS
RELATIONSHIP BUILDING SUMMARY

Describe the new learning in a quick summary. Then note the action plan with each new relationship. Add it to your weekly summary with an **RB** for the category code.

#	NAME	GROUP	ACTION PLAN
1			
2			
3			
4			
5			
6			
7			
8			
9			
10			
11			
12			
13			
14			
15			
16			
17			
18			
19			
20			

NEW JOB SUCCESS CHALLENGES

Describe the new learning in a quick summary. Then note the action plan with each challenge.
Add it to your weekly summary with the appropriate challenge code; **F | C | A | PN**

#	CODE	DESCRIPTION	ACTION PLAN
1			
2			
3			
4			
5			
6			
7			
8			
9			
10			
11			
12			
13			
14			
15			
16			
17			
18			
19			
20			

NEW JOB SUCCESS GOALS SUMMARY

Describe the new learning in a quick summary. Then note the action plan for each goal.
Add it to your weekly summary with **G** as the category code..

#	GOAL	ACTION PLAN
13		
14		
15		
16		
17		
18		
19		
20		
21		
22		
23		
24		

NEW JOB SUCCESS BALANCING ACT SUMMARY

Describe the new learning in a quick summary. Then note the action plan with each activity.
Add it to your weekly summary with **BA** for the category code..

#	DESCRIPTION	ACTION PLAN
13		
14		
15		
16		
17		
18		
19		
20		
21		
22		
23		
24		

Conclusion

That's it! After one year in your new job, you should be able to implement all the subjects discussed in this book. It seems like a lot, but everything will go smoothly, and one thing leads to another if you know where you're going and what you need to do. In the introduction, I shared the Learning Competency Model, which focuses on moving to high levels of competence. That model guided the layout of this book, and hopefully, you have seen the results.

Remember, this book is not just a one-time read. It's a reference guide that you can turn to throughout your first year and beyond. To recap:

The first thing we discussed was demonstrating and delivering value, and I have highlighted how important that is when you start a new job. Here, you have to set clear goals through KPIs to quantify the impact you're making successfully. Remember the four-step model—plan, execute, assess, and communicate. This is an excellent approach to showcasing your contributions. Communicating and effective reporting are crucial so you can convey your achievements to others and help them realize the value you bring to the company.

It is also true that in the first few months, you have to learn fast to get up to speed, and even after that, you should use the skills learned here to continue to absorb more knowledge as quickly as you can, not only in the first three months of your new job. You must assess your existing knowledge, identify the gaps, and focus on the most critical areas. You must also determine your preferred learning style and use techniques like the Pomodoro technique, which can help you learn things faster and more efficiently.

Remember, success in your new workplace isn't just about hard work. It's also about building relationships. Empathy, effective communication, and active listening are all keys to fostering meaningful connections with your colleagues. We've explored various strategies, such as engaging in small talk and asking questions, to help you grow your professional network. These strategies and the skills you develop will help you establish valuable relationships with everyone around you, fostering a more collaborative work environment.

Your first year will undoubtedly bring some common challenges, such as the fear of failure, conflict, ambiguity, and keeping up with workload management. However, communication is a big part of overcoming such challenges. We've discussed a few approaches that might help you, such as radical candor, crucial conversations, or nonviolent communication. This includes models that help you overcome these challenges, such as the different negotiation approaches or the agile and sprint models. Remember that success can also be a challenge because it shouldn't be a one-time achievement; you must continue. For that, you should remember to celebrate your accomplishments, big or small; this will boost your confidence and increase your motivation. Failure is another challenge that you might face in your first year and definitely later on, but you must remember that it is a natural part of professional growth. You have to embrace failures and see them as learning opportunities. Much like failures, conflicts are inevitable, but by using the communication approaches I have highlighted above, you will find a solution for them. Ambiguity is a reasonably common challenge in the workplace, and iterative communication and agile and sprint approaches are great tools to overcome this. Remember to break tasks into manageable chunks so you can keep moving forward.

Your image and brand are what people around you will see, and you have to be able to align them with your authentic personal brand if you want to continue to grow professionally. You must balance everything and achieve equilibrium between your personal and professional lives. We've looked at the importance of self-care and self-reflection, prioritizing your physical, mental, social, emotional, and spiritual well-being that will contribute to a fulfilled life, and how you can achieve that.

Lastly, I have talked about keeping a journal so you can track your progress, set goals, and apply the concepts we've talked about in your workplace. This tool will provide you with a structure you can follow and accountability that will help you stay focused and perform your daily tasks effectively.

As you continue your professional career, I always tell my clients that growth is an ongoing process; there's always more to learn, and we can continually improve. Embrace each day as an opportunity to do better, to understand and build relationships, to overcome challenges, and to achieve success. A career is never a straight line; it comes with left and right turns. But that is part of the growth and adventure, and there will be setbacks and victories. I urge and encourage you to keep focused and balanced. That attitude and the ideas in this book give you a strong foundation for your rewarding journey ahead.

Acknowledgements

This book has been a wonderful journey to create and I have a community to thank, starting with my wife Antonette and son Andy. They are my absolute foundations and North Stars.

My coaching clients and students who teach and guide me more than they realize. Through their trust in me and our collaboration, we built out the ideas and model for this book. Their success and journeys are in each page of this book.

Art Director Yayun Chang Cahill balances an incredible artistic eye with business pragmatism, even when I veer off the brand. My amazing Hudson Coaching Book Club: Margaret Enloe, Jackie Verity and Candice Weber, their feedback and positive vibes added a lot. Margaret provided deep, thoughtful edits that provided much needed clarification. My editor Hillary Read has been amazing at keeping not just the book, but my overall content targeted and impactful.

And finally, the community I founded The Career Circles. A place where members can grow their career along with the help of a vibrant, helpful group.

References

Adams, L. (2011, July). Learning a New Skill is Easier Said Than Done https://www.gordontraining.com/free-workplace-articles/learning-a-new-skill-is-easier-said-than-done/

Angeline, M. (2022, July 21). 7 steps to effective workload planning. Runn. https://www.runn.io/blog/workload-planning

Basiouny, A. (2022, March 29). How to have more successful conversations. Knowledge at Wharton. https://knowledge.wharton.upenn.edu/article/how-to-have-more-successful-conversations/

Bernardoni, A. (2022, November 22). Managing ambiguity in the workplace. Hanover Search. https://www.hanoversearch.com/blogs/2021-11/how-to-manage-ambiguity-in-the-workplace

Business Broken Down team. (2016, January 18). How to motivate yourself in times of failure. Business Broken Down. https://businessbrokendown.com/2016/01/18/how-to-motivate-yourself-in-times-of-failure/

ClearInfo team. (2022, January 3). Business communication report writing. Clearinfo. https://clearinfo.in/blog/business-communication-report-writing/

Collins, B. (2020, March 3). The pomodoro technique explained. Forbes. https://www.forbes.com/sites/bryancollinseurope/2020/03/03/the-pomodoro-technique/

Dexian team. (2023, April 24). Creating a failure-safe workplace. Dexian. https://dexian.com/blog/do-your-employees-feel-safe-enough-to-fail-5-ways-leaders-can-create-a-failure-safe-workplace/

Hayes, A. (2023, July 24). Gap analysis. Investopedia. https://www.investopedia.com/terms/g/gap-analysis.asp#:~:text=A%20gap%20analysis%20is%20the

Hennigan, L. (2023, April 24). What is A KPI? Definition & examples. Forbes. https://www.forbes.com/advisor/business/what-is-a-kpi-definition-examples/

Mannering, L. (2019, September 17). The awkward but essential art of office chitchat. The New York Times. https://www.nytimes.com/2019/09/17/style/the-awkward-art-of-office-small-talk.html

Mayo Clinic Staff. (2020, April 17). 6 steps to better sleep. Mayo Clinic. https://www.mayoclinic.org/healthy-lifestyle/adult-health/in-depth/sleep/art-20048379

Millard, M. (2023, January 15). Driving progress: How to promote continuous improvement in the workplace. Blog.kainexus. https://blog.kainexus.com/continuous-improvement/culture-of-continuous-improvement/7-surefire-ways-to-promote-continuous-improvement-in-the-workplace

Mind team. (2019). Wellbeing. Mind.org.uk. https://www.mind.org.uk/information-support/tips-for-everyday-living/wellbeing/

Orduña, N. (2022, September 28). How to build your personal brand at work. Harvard Business Review. https://hbr.org/2022/09/how-to-build-your-personal-brand-at-work

Profit Co team. (2022, April 18). What are FAST goals? How are they better than SMART goals? Best OKR Software by Profit.co. https://www.profit.co/blog/okr-university/what-are-fast-goals-how-are-t

hey-better-than-smart-goals/#:~:text=FAST%20goals%20stand%20for%20Frequently

Rossingol, N. (2022, May 5). Radical candor: a book summary chapter by chapter | runn. Runn. https://www.runn.io/blog/radical-candor-summary#chapter-1

Sanfilippo, M. (2023). How to improve your work-life balance. Business News Daily. https://www.businessnewsdaily.com/5244-improve-work-life-balance-today.html

StuderEducation Content Team. (2019, June 12). Process improvement tool: Stoplight report. Studer Education. https://www.studereducation.com/process-improvement-tools-tool-6-stoplight-report/

Temple, B. (2022, July 3). How to keep a work journal. Visualcv. https://www.visualcv.com/blog/how-to-keep-a-work-journal/

Twin, A. (2023, May 10). Understanding key performance indicators (KPI). Investopedia. https://www.investopedia.com/terms/k/kpi.asp

Waters, S. (2022, May 3). Building good work relationships and all of the benefits. Betterup. https://www.betterup.com/blog/building-good-work-relationships

About the Author

Mike has worn many hats in his career; he's an author and certified executive coach who spent over two decades as a recruiting leader and has been an acclaimed program leader at the world-renowned Wharton Business School. In his career, Mike has helped thousands of professionals, many on a one-to-one basis, navigate the ever-evolving landscape of the workplace.

Mike empowers individuals to unlock their full career potential by leveraging his experience, empathy, and knowledge to help people discover their own unique paths.

A certified coach with the International Coaching Federation, Mike is also a successful startup founder and leader in both Healthcare and Tech. Mike co-authored The Job Search Manifesto with Steve Hernandez. He has a degree in Health Information Systems from Seattle University with an emphasis in Psychology and Nursing.

You can learn more about Mike from his personal website MikeCoach.com or his community site The Career Circle.com

A Final Word on Reviews

I wanted to share this again. Book Reviews are the core of an author's success. Take a moment to do this. I am grateful for all the feedback. It boosts the popularity of the book by helping other readers with their careers. Here are the links:

Amazon US| Amazon Canada | Amazon UK | Amazon Germany | Amazon France | Amazon Spain | Amazon Netherlands

In advance, thank you! Your review expands this book's reach. More reviews means more readers who can grow and succeed in their career.

Thank you!

Made in the USA
Columbia, SC
25 January 2025